MARUJA

BRET HARTE

1st WORLD
LIBRARY
Literary Society

Maruja

Bret Harte

© 1st World Library, 2008
PO Box 2211
Fairfield, IA 52556
www.1stworldlibrary.com
First Edition

LCCN: 2007935356

Softcover ISBN: 978-1-4218-9311-2
Hardcover ISBN: 978-1-4218-9411-9
eBook ISBN: 978-1-4218-9211-5

Purchase *"Maruja"*
as a traditional bound book at:
www.1stWorldLibrary.com/purchase.asp?ISBN=978-1-4218-9311-2

1st World Library is a literary, educational organization
dedicated to:

- Creating a free internet library of downloadable ebooks

- Hosting writing competitions and offering book publishing scholarships.

Interested in more 1st World Library books? contact:
literacy@1stworldlibrary.com
Check us out at: www.1stworldlibrary.com

1st World Library Literary Society

Giving Back to the World

"If you want to work on the core problem, it's early school literacy."

- James Barksdale, former CEO of Netscape

"No skill is more crucial to the future of a child, or to a democratic and prosperous society, than literacy."

- Los Angeles Times

"Literacy... means far more than learning how to read and write... The aim is to transmit... knowledge and promote social participation."

- UNESCO

"Literacy is not a luxury, it is a right and a responsibility. If our world is to meet the challenges of the twenty-first century we must harness the energy and creativity of all our citizens."

- President Bill Clinton

"Parents should be encouraged to read to their children, and teachers should be equipped with all available techniques for teaching literacy, so the varying needs and capacities of individual kids can be taken into account."

- Hugh Mackay

CHAPTER I

Morning was breaking on the high road to San Jose. The long lines of dusty, level track were beginning to extend their vanishing point in the growing light; on either side the awakening fields of wheat and oats were stretching out and broadening to the sky. In the east and south the stars were receding before the coming day; in the west a few still glimmered, caught among the bosky hills of the canada del Raimundo, where night seemed to linger. Thither some obscure, low-flying birds were slowly winging; thither a gray coyote, overtaken by the morning, was awkwardly limping. And thither a tramping wayfarer turned, plowing through the dust of the highway still unslaked by the dewless night, to climb the fence and likewise seek the distant cover.

For some moments man and beast kept an equal pace and gait with a strange similarity of appearance and expression; the coyote bearing that resemblance to his more civilized and harmless congener, the dog, which the tramp bore to the ordinary pedestrians, but both exhibiting the same character-istics of lazy vagabondage and semi-lawlessness; the coyote's slouching amble and uneasy stealthiness being repeated in the tramp's shuffling step and sidelong glances. Both were young, and physically vigorous, but both displayed the same vacillating and awkward disinclination to direct effort. They continued thus half a mile apart unconscious of each other, until the superior faculties of the brute warned him of the contiguity of aggressive civilization, and he cantered off suddenly to the right, fully five minutes before the barking of dogs caused the man to make a detour to the left to avoid entrance upon a cultivated domain that lay before him.

The trail he took led to one of the scant water-courses that issued, half spent, from the canada, to fade out utterly on the hot June plain. It was thickly bordered with willows and alders, that made an arbored and feasible path through the dense woods and undergrowth. He continued along it as if aimlessly; stopping from time to time to look at different objects in a dull mechanical fashion, as if rather to prolong his useless hours, than from any curious instinct, and to occasionally dip in the unfrequent pools of water the few crusts of bread he had taken from his pocket. Even this appeared to be suggested more by coincidence of material in the bread and water, than from the promptings of hunger. At last he reached a cup-like hollow in the hills lined with wild clover and thick with resinous odors. Here he crept under a manzanita-bush and disposed himself to sleep. The act showed he was already familiar with the local habits of his class, who used the unfailing dry starlit nights for their wanderings, and spent the hours of glaring sunshine asleep or resting in some wayside shadow.

Meanwhile the light quickened, and gradually disclosed the form and outline of the adjacent domain. An avenue cut through a park-like wood, carefully cleared of the under-growth of gigantic ferns peculiar to the locality, led to the entrance of the canada. Here began a vast terrace of lawn, broken up by enormous bouquets of flower-beds bewildering in color and profusion, from which again rose the flowering vines and trailing shrubs that hid pillars, veranda, and even the long facade of a great and dominant mansion. But the delicacy of floral outlines running to the capitals of columns and at times mounting to the pediment of the roof, the opulence of flashing color or the massing of tropical foliage, could not deprive it of the imperious dignity of size and space. Much of this was due to the fact that the original casa —an adobe house of no mean pretensions, dating back to the early Spanish occupation—had been kept intact, sheathed in a shell of dark-red wood, and still retaining its patio; or inner court-yard, surrounded by low galleries, while additions, greater in extent than the main building, had been erected— not as wings and projections, but massed upon it on either side, changing its rigid square outlines to a vague parallelo- gram. While the patio retained the Spanish conception of al fresco seclusion, a vast colonnade of veranda on the southern side was a concession to American taste, and its breadth gave that depth of shadow to the inner rooms which had been lost in the thinner shell of the new erection. Its cloistered gloom was lightened by the red fires of cardinal flowers dropping from the roof, by the yellow sunshine of the jessamine creeping up the columns, by billows of heliotropes breaking over its base as a purple sea. Nowhere else did the opulence of this climate of blossoms show itself as vividly. Even the Castilian roses, that grew as vines along the east front, the fuchsias, that attained the dignity of trees, in the patio, or the four or five monster passion-vines that bestarred the low western wall, and told over and over again their mystic story—paled before the sensuous glory of the south veranda.

As the sun arose, that part of the quiet house first touched by its light seemed to waken. A few lounging peons and servants made their appearance at the entrance of the patio, occasionally reinforced by an earlier life from the gardens and stables. But the south facade of the building had not apparently gone to bed at all: lights were still burning dimly in the large ball-room; a tray with glasses stood upon the veranda near one of the open French windows, and further on, a half-shut yellow fan lay like a fallen leaf. The sound of carriage-wheels on the gravel terrace brought with it voices and laughter and the swiftly passing vision of a char-a-bancs filled with muffled figures bending low to avoid the direct advances of the sun.

As the carriage rolled away, four men lounged out of a window on the veranda, shading their eyes against the level beams. One was still in evening dress, and one in the uniform of a captain of artillery; the others had already changed their gala attire, the elder of the party having assumed those extravagant tweeds which the tourist from Great Britain usually offers as a gentle concession to inferior yet more florid civilization. Nevertheless, he beamed back heartily on the sun, and remarked, in a pleasant Scotch accent, that: Did they know it was very extraordinary how clear the morning was, so free from clouds and mist and fog? The young man in evening dress fluently agreed to the facts, and suggested, in idiomatic French-English, that one comprehended that the bed was an insult to one's higher nature and an ingratitude to their gracious hostess, who had spread out this lovely garden and walks for their pleasure; that nothing was more beautiful than the dew sparkling on the rose, or the matin song of the little birds.

The other young man here felt called upon to point out the fact that there was no dew in California, and that the birds did not sing in that part of the country. The foreign young gentleman received this statement with pain and astonishment as to the fact, with passionate remorse as to his own ignorance. But still, as it was a charming day, would not his gallant friend, the Captain here, accept the challenge of the brave Englishman, and "walk him" for the glory of his flag and a thousand pounds?

The gallant Captain, unfortunately, believed that if he

Bret Harte

walked out in his uniform he would suffer some delay from being interrogated by wayfarers as to the locality of the circus he would be pleasantly supposed to represent, even if he escaped being shot as a rare California bird by the foreign sporting contingent. In these circumstances, he would simply lounge around the house until his carriage was ready.

Much as it pained him to withdraw from such amusing companions, the foreign young gentleman here felt that he, too, would retire for the present to change his garments, and glided back through the window at the same moment that the young officer carelessly stepped from the veranda and lounged towards the shrubbery.

"They've been watching each other for the last hour. I wonder what's up?" said the young man who remained.

The remark, without being confidential, was so clearly the first sentence of natural conversation that the Scotchman, although relieved, said, "Eh, man?" a little cautiously.

"It's as clear as this sunshine that Captain Carroll and Garnier are each particularly anxious to know what the other is doing or intends to do this morning."

"Why did they separate, then?" asked the other.

"That's a mere blind. Garnier's looking through his window now at Carroll, and Carroll is aware of it."

"Eh!" said the Scotchman, with good-humored curiosity. "Is it a quarrel? Nothing serious, I hope. No revolvers and bowie-knives, man, before breakfast, eh?"

"No," laughed the younger man. "No! To do Maruja justice, she generally makes a fellow too preposterous to fight. I see you don't understand. You're a stranger; I'm an old habitue of the house—let me explain. Both of these men are in love with Maruja; or, worse than that, they firmly believe her to be in love with THEM."

"But Miss Maruja is the eldest daughter of our hostess, is she not?" said the Scotchman; "and I understood from one of the young ladies that the Captain had come down from the Fort particularly to pay court to Miss Amita, the beauty."

"Possibly. But that wouldn't prevent Maruja from flirting with him."

"Eh! but are you not mistaken, Mr. Raymond? Certainly a more quiet, modest, and demure young lassie I never met."

"That's because she sat out two waltzes with you, and let you do the talking, while she simply listened."

The elder man's fresh color for an instant heightened, but he recovered himself with a good-humored laugh. "Likely—likely. She's a capital good listener."

"You're not the first man that found her eloquent. Stanton, your banking friend, who never talks of anything but mines and stocks, says she's the only woman who has any conversation; and we can all swear that she never said two words to him the whole time she sat next to him at dinner. But she looked at him as if she had. Why, man, woman, and child all give her credit for any grace that pleases themselves. And why? Because she's clever enough not to practice any one of them—as graces. I don't know the girl that claims less and gets more. For instance, you don't call her pretty?"

"Wait a bit. Ye'll not get on so fast, my young friend; I'm not

Bret Harte

prepared to say that she's not," returned the Scotchman, with good-humored yet serious caution.

"But you would have been prepared yesterday, and have said it. She can produce the effect of the prettiest girl here, and without challenging comparison. Nobody thinks of her—everybody experiences her."

"You're an enthusiast, Mr. Raymond. As an habitue of the house, of course, you—"

"Oh, my time came with the rest," laughed the young man, with unaffected frankness. "It's about two years ago now."

"I see—you were not a marrying man."

"Pardon me—it was because I was."

The Scotchman looked at him curiously.

"Maruja is an heiress. I am a mining engineer."

"But, my dear fellow, I thought that in your country—"

"In MY country, yes. But we are standing on a bit of old Spain. This land was given to Dona Maria Saltonstall's ancestors by Charles V. Look around you. This veranda, this larger shell of the ancient casa, is the work of the old Salem whaling captain that she married, and is all that is American here. But the heart of the house, as well as the life that circles around the old patio, is Spanish. The Dona's family, the Estudillos and Guitierrez, always looked down upon this alliance with the Yankee captain, though it brought improvement to the land, and increased its value forty-fold, and since his death ever opposed any further foreign intervention. Not that that would weigh much with Maruja if she took a fancy to any one; Spanish as she is throughout, in thought and grace and feature, there is enough of the old Salem witches' blood in her to defy law and authority in following an unhallowed worship. There are no sons; she is the sole heiress of the house and estate—though, according to the native custom, her sisters will be separately portioned from the other property, which is very large."

"Then the Captain might still make a pretty penny on Amita," said the Scotchman.

"If he did not risk and lose it all on Maruja. There is enough of the old Spanish jealousy in the blood to make even the gentle Amita never forgive his momentary defection."

Something in his manner made the Scotchman think that Raymond spoke from baleful experience. How else could this attractive young fellow, educated abroad and a rising man in his profession, have failed to profit by his contiguity to such advantages, and the fact of his being an evident favorite?

"But with this opposition on the part of the relatives to any further alliances with your countrymen, why does our hostess expose her daughters to their fascinating influence?" said the elder man, glancing at his companion. "The girls seem to have the usual American freedom."

"Perhaps they are therefore the less likely to give it up to the first man who asks them. But the Spanish duenna still survives in the family—the more awful because invisible. It's a mysterious fact that as soon as a fellow becomes particularly attached to any one—except Maruja—he receives some intimation from Pereo."

"What! the butler? That Indian-looking fellow? A servant?"

"Pardon me—the mayordomo. The old confidential servitor who stands in loco parentis. No one knows what he says. If the victim appeals to the mistress, she is indisposed; you know she has such bad health. If in his madness he makes a confidante of Maruja, that finishes him."

"How?"

"Why, he ends by transferring his young affections to her—with the usual result."

"Then you don't think our friend the Captain has had this confidential butler ask his intentions yet?"

"I don't think it will be necessary," said the other, dryly.

"Umph! Meantime, the Captain has just vanished through yon shrubbery. I suppose that's the end of the mysterious espionage you have discovered. No! De'il take it! but there's that Frenchman popping out of the myrtlebush. How did the fellow get there? And, bless me! here's our lassie, too!"

"Yes!" said Raymond, in a changed voice, "It's Maruja!"

She had approached so noiselessly along the bank that bordered the veranda, gliding from pillar to pillar as she paused before each to search for some particular flower, that both men felt an uneasy consciousness. But she betrayed no indication of their presence by look or gesture. So absorbed and abstracted she seemed that, by a common instinct, they both drew nearer the window, and silently waited for her to pass or recognize them.

She halted a few paces off to fasten a flower in her girdle. A small youthful figure, in a pale yellow dress, lacking even the maturity of womanly outline. The full oval of her face, the straight line of her back, a slight boyishness in the contour of her hips, the infantine smallness of her sandaled feet and narrow hands, were all suggestive of fresh, innocent, amiable youth—and nothing more.

Forgetting himself, the elder man mischievously crushed his companion against the wall in mock virtuous indignation. "Eh, sir," he whispered, with an accent that broadened with his feelings. "Eh, but look at the puir wee lassie! Will ye no be ashamed o' yerself for putting the tricks of a Circe on sic a honest gentle bairn? Why, man, you'll be seein' the sign of a limb of Satan in a bit thing with the mother's milk not yet out of her! She a flirt, speerin' at men, with that modest downcast air? I'm ashamed of ye, Mister Raymond. She's only thinking of her breakfast, puir thing, and not of yon callant. Another sacrilegious word and I'll expose you to her. Have ye no pity on youth and innocence?"

"Let me up," groaned Raymond, feebly, "and I'll tell you how old she is. Hush—she's looking."

The two men straightened themselves. She had, indeed, lifted her eyes towards the window. They were beautiful eyes, and charged with something more than their own beauty. With a deep brunette setting even to the darkened cornea, the pupils were blue as the sky above them. But they were lit with another intelligence. The soul of the Salem whaler looked out of the passion-darkened orbits of the mother, and was resistless.

She smiled recognition of the two men with sedate girlishness and a foreign inclination of the head over the flowers she was holding. Her straight, curveless mouth became suddenly charming with the parting of her lips over her white teeth, and left the impress of the smile in a lighting of the whole face even after it had passed. Then she moved away. At the same moment Garnier approached her.

"Come away, man, and have our walk," said the Scotchman, seizing Raymond's arm. "We'll not spoil that fellow's sport."

"No; but she will, I fear. Look, Mr. Buchanan, if she hasn't given him her flowers to carry to the house while she waits here for the Captain!"

"Come away, scoffer!" said Buchanan, good-humoredly, locking his arm in the young man's and dragging him from the veranda towards the avenue, "and keep your observations for breakfast."

CHAPTER II

In the mean time, the young officer, who had disappeared in the shrubbery, whether he had or had not been a spectator of the scene, exhibited some signs of agitation. He walked rapidly on, occasionally switching the air with a wand of willow, from which he had impatiently plucked the leaves, through an alley of ceanothus, until he reached a little thicket of evergreens, which seemed to oppose his further progress. Turning to one side, however, he quickly found an entrance to a labyrinthine walk, which led him at last to an open space and a rustic summer-house that stood beneath a gnarled and venerable pear-tree. The summerhouse was a quaint stockade of dark madrono boughs thatched with red-wood bark, strongly suggestive of deeper woodland shadow. But in strange contrast, the floor, table, and benches were thickly strewn with faded rose-leaves, scattered as if in some riotous play of children. Captain Carroll brushed them aside hurriedly with his impatient foot, glanced around hastily, then threw himself on the rustic bench at full length and twisted his mustache between his nervous fingers. Then he rose as suddenly, with a few white petals impaled on his gilded spurs and stepped quickly into the open sunlight.

He must have been mistaken! Everything was quiet around him, the far-off sound of wheels in the avenue came faintly, but nothing more.

Bret Harte

His eye fell upon the pear-tree, and even in his preoccupation he was struck with the signs of its extraordinary age. Twisted out of all proportion, and knotted with excrescences, it was supported by iron bands and heavy stakes, as if to prop up its senile decay. He tried to interest himself in the various initials and symbols deeply carved in bark, now swollen and half obliterated. As he turned back to the summer-house, he for the first time noticed that the ground rose behind it into a long undulation, on the crest of which the same singular profusion of rose-leaves were scattered. It struck him as being strangely like a gigantic grave, and that the same idea had occurred to the fantastic dispenser of the withered flowers. He was still looking at it, when a rustle in the undergrowth made his heart beat expectantly. A slinking gray shadow crossed the undulation and disappeared in the thicket. It was a coyote. At any other time the extraordinary appearance of this vivid impersonation of the wilderness, so near a centre of human civilization and habitation, would have filled him with wonder. But he had room for only a single thought now. Would SHE come?

Five minutes passed. He no longer waited in the summer-house, but paced impatiently before the entrance to the labyrinth. Another five minutes. He was deceived, undoubtedly. She and her sisters were probably waiting for him and laughing at him on the lawn. He ground his heel into the clover, and threw his switch into the thicket. Yet he would give her one—only one moment more.

"Captain Carroll!"

The voice had been and was to HIM the sweetest in the world; but even a stranger could not have resisted the spell of its musical inflection. He turned quickly. She was advancing towards him from the summer-house.

"Did you think I was coming that way—where everybody could follow me?" she laughed, softly. "No; I came through the thicket over there," indicating the direction with her flexible shoulder, "and nearly lost my slipper and my eyes—look!" She threw back the inseparable lace shawl from her blond head, and showed a spray of myrtle clinging like a broken wreath to her forehead. The young officer remained gazing at her silently.

"I like to hear you speak my name," he said, with a slight hesitation in his breath. "Say it again."

"Car-roll, Car-roll, Car-roll," she murmured gently to herself two or three times, as if enjoying her own native trilling of the r's. "It's a pretty name. It sounds like a song. Don Carroll, eh! El Capitan Don Carroll."

"But my first name is Henry," he said, faintly.

"'Enry—that's not so good. Don Enrico will do. But El Capitan Carroll is best of all. I must have it always: El Capitan Carroll!"

"Always?" He colored like a boy.

"Why not?" He was confusedly trying to look through her brown lashes; she was parrying him with the steel of her father's glance. "Come! Well! Captain Carroll! It was not to tell me your name—that I knew already was pretty—Car-roll!" she murmured again, caressing him with her lashes; "it was not for this that you asked me to meet you face to face in this—cold"—she made a movement of drawing her lace over her shoulders—"cold daylight. That belonged to the lights and the dance and the music of last night. It is not for this you expect me to leave my guests, to run away from Monsieur Garnier, who pays compliments, but whose name is not pretty—from Mr. Raymond, who talks OF me when he can't talk TO me. They will say, This Captain Carroll could say all that before them."

"But if they knew," said the young officer, drawing closer to her with a paling face but brightening eyes, "if they knew I had anything else to say, Miss Saltonstall—something—pardon me—did I hurt your hand?—something for HER alone—is there one of them that would have the right to object? Do not think me foolish, Miss Saltonstall—but—I beg—I implore you to tell me before I say more."

"Who would have a right?" said Maruja, withdrawing her hand but not her dangerous eyes. "Who would dare forbid you talking to me of my sister? I have told you that Amita is free—as we all are."

Captain Carroll fell back a few steps and gazed at her with a troubled face. "It is possible that you have misunderstood, Miss Saltonstall?" he faltered. "Do you still think it is Amita that I"—he stopped and added passionately, "Do you remember what I told you?—have you forgotten last night?"

"Last night was—last night!" said Maruja, slightly lifting her shoulders. "One makes love at night—one marries in day-light. In the music, in the flowers, in the moonlight, one says everything; in the morning one has breakfast—when one is not asked to have councils of war with captains and commandantes. You would speak of my sister, Captain Car-roll—go on. Dona Amita Carroll sounds very, very pretty. I shall not object." She held out both her hands to him, threw her head back, and smiled.

He seized her hands passionately. "No, no! you shall hear me—you shall understand me. I love YOU, Maruja—you, and you alone. God knows I can not help it— God knows I would not help it if I could. Hear me. I will be calm. No one can hear us where we stand. I am not mad. I am not a traitor! I frankly admired your sister. I came here to see her. Beyond that, I swear to you, I am guiltless to her—to you. Even she knows no more of me than that. I saw you, Maruja. From that moment I have thought of nothing—dreamed of nothing else."

"That is—three, four, five days and one afternoon ago! You see, I remember. And now you want—what?"

"To let me love you, and you only. To let me be with you. To let me win you in time, as you should be won. I am not mad, though I am desperate. I know what is due to your station and mine—even while I dare to say I love you. Let me hope, Maruja, I only ask to hope."

She looked at him until she had absorbed all the burning fever of his eyes, until her ears tingled with his passionate voice, and then—she shook her head.

"It can not be, Carroll—no! never!"

He drew himself up under the blow with such simple and manly dignity that her eyes dropped for the moment. "There is another, then?" he said, sadly.

"There is no one I care for better than you. No! Do not be foolish. Let me go. I tell you that because you can be nothing to me—you understand, to ME. To my sister Amita, yes."

The young soldier raised his head coldly. "I have pressed you hard, Miss Saltonstall—too hard, I know, for a man who has already had his answer; but I did not deserve this. Good-by."

"Stop," she said, gently. "I meant not to hurt you, Captain

Carroll. If I had, it is not thus I would have done. I need not have met you here. Would you have loved me the less if I had avoided this meeting?"

He could not reply. In the depths of his miserable heart, he knew that he would have loved her the same.

"Come," she said, laying her hand softly on his arm, "do not be angry with me for putting you back only five days to where you were when you first entered our house. Five days is not much of happiness or sorrow to forget, is it, Carroll—Captain Carroll?" Her voice died away in a faint sigh. "Do not be angry with me, if—knowing you could be nothing more—I wanted you to love my sister, and my sister to love you. We should have been good friends—such good friends."

"Why do you say, 'Knowing it could he nothing more'?" said Carroll, grasping her hand suddenly. "In the name of Heaven, tell me what you mean!"

"I mean I can not marry unless I marry one of my mother's race. That is my mother's wish, and the will of her relations. You are an American, not of Spanish blood."

"But surely this is not your determination?"

She shrugged her shoulders. "What would you? It is the determination of my people."

"But knowing this"—he stopped; the quick blood rose to his face.

"Go on, Captain Carroll. You would say, Knowing this, why did I not warn you? Why did I not say to you when we first met, You have come to address my sister; do not fall in love with me—I can not marry a foreigner."

"You are cruel, Maruja. But, if that is all, surely this prejudice can be removed? Why, your mother married a foreigner—an American."

"Perhaps that is why," said the girl, quietly. She cast down her long lashes, and with the point of her satin slipper smoothed out the soft leaves of the clover at her feet. "Listen; shall I tell you the story of our house? Stop! some one is coming. Don't move; remain as you are. If you care for me, Carroll, collect yourself, and don't let that man think he has found US ridiculous." Her voice changed from its tone of slight caressing pleading to one of suppressed pride. "HE will not laugh much, Captain Carroll; truly, no."

The figure of Garnier, bright, self-possessed, courteous, appeared at the opening of the labyrinth. Too well-bred to suggest, even in complimentary raillery, a possible senti- mental situation, his politeness went further. It was so kind in them to guide an awkward stranger by their voices to the places where he could not stupidly intrude!

"You are just in time to interrupt or to hear a story that I have been threatening to tell," she said, composedly; "an old Spanish legend of this house. You are in the majority now, you two, and can stop me if you choose. Thank you. I warn you it is stupid; it isn't new; but it has the excuse of being suggested by this very spot." She cast a quick look of subtle meaning at Carroll, and throughout her recital appealed more directly to him, in a manner delicately yet sufficiently marked to partly soothe his troubled spirit.

"Far back, in the very old times, Caballeros," said Maruja, standing by the table in mock solemnity, and rapping upon it with her fan, "this place was the home of the coyote. Big and little, father and mother, Senor and Senora Coyotes, and the little muchacho coyotes had their home in the dark canada, and came out over these fields, yellow with wild oats and red with poppies, to seek their prey. They were happy. For why? They were the first; they had no history, you comprehend, no tradition. They married as they liked" (with a glance at Carroll), "nobody objected; they increased and multiplied. But the plains were fertile; the game was plentiful; it was not fit that it should be for the beasts alone. And so, in the course of time, an Indian chief, a heathen, Koorotora, built his wigwam here."

"I beg your pardon," said Garnier, in apparent distress, "but I caught the gentleman's name imperfectly."

Fully aware that the questioner only wished to hear again her musical enunciation of the consonants, she repeated, "Koorotora," with an apologetic glance at Carroll, and went on. "This gentleman had no history or tradition to bother him, either; whatever Senor Coyote thought of the matter, he contented himself with robbing Senor Koorotora's wigwam when he could, and skulking around the Indian's camp at night. The old chief prospered, and made many journeys round the country, but always kept his camp here. This lasted until the time when the holy Fathers came from the South, and Portala, as you have all read, uplifted the wooden Cross on the sea-coast over there, and left it for the heathens to wonder at. Koorotora saw it on one of his journeys, and came back to the canada full of this wonder. Now, Koorotora had a wife."

"Ah, we shall commence now. We are at the beginning. This is better than Senora Coyota," said Garnier, cheerfully.

"Naturally, she was anxious to see the wonderful object. She saw it, and she saw the holy Fathers, and they converted her against the superstitious heathenish wishes of her husband. And more than that, they came here—"

"And converted the land also; is it not so? It was a lovely site for a mission," interpolated Garnier, politely.

"They built a mission and brought as many of Koorotora's people as they could into the sacred fold. They brought them in in a queer fashion sometimes, it is said; dragoons from the Presidio, Captain Carroll, lassoing them and bringing them in at the tails of their horses. All except Koorotora. He defied them; he cursed them and his wife in his wicked heathenish fashion, and said that they too should lose the mission through the treachery of some woman, and that the coyote should yet prowl through the ruined walls of the church. The holy Fathers pitied the wicked man—and built themselves a lovely garden. Look at that pear-tree! There is all that is left of it!"

She turned with a mock heroic gesture, and pointed her fan to the pear-tree. Garnier lifted his hands in equally simulated wonder. A sudden recollection of the coyote of the morning recurred to Carroll uneasily. "And the Indians," he said, with an effort to shake off the feeling; "they, too, have vanished."

"All that remained of them is in yonder mound. It is the grave of the chief and his people. He never lived to see the fulfillment of his prophecy. For it was a year after his death that our ancestor, Manuel Guitierrez, came from old Spain to the Presidio with a grant of twenty leagues to settle where he chose. Dona Maria Guitierrez took a fancy to the canada. But it was a site already in possession of the Holy Church. One night, through treachery, it was said, the guards were withdrawn and the Indians entered the mission, slaughtered the lay brethren, and drove away the priests. The Commandant at the Presidio retook the place from the heathens, but on representation to the Governor that it was indefensible for the peaceful Fathers without a large military guard, the official ordered the removal of the mission to Santa Cruz, and Don Manuel settled his twenty leagues grant in the canada. Whether he or Dona Maria had anything to do with the Indian uprising, no one knows; but Father Pedro never forgave them. He is said to have declared at the foot of the altar that the curse of the Church was on the land, and that it should always pass into the hands of the stranger."

"And that was long ago, and the property is still in the family," said Carroll, hurriedly, answering Maruja's eyes.

"In the last hundred years there have been no male heirs," continued Maruja, still regarding Carroll. "When my mother, who was the eldest daughter, married Don Jose Saltonstall against the wishes of the family, it was said that the curse would fall. Sure enough, Caballeros, it was that year that the forged grants of Micheltorrena were discovered; and in our lawsuit your government, Captain, handed over ten leagues of the llano land to the Doctor West, our neighbor."

"Ah, the gray-headed gentleman who lunched here the other day? You are friends, then? You bear no malice?" said Garnier.

"What would you?" said Maruja, with a slight shrug of her shoulders. "He paid his money to the forger. Your corregidores upheld him, and said it was no forgery," she continued, to Carroll.

In spite of the implied reproach, Carroll felt relieved. He began to be impatient of Garnier's presence, and longed to renew his suit. Perhaps his face showed something of this, for Maruja added, with mock demureness, "It's always dreadful to be the eldest sister; but think what it is to be in the direct line of a curse! Now, there's Amita—SHE'S free to do as she likes, with no family responsibility; while poor me!" She dropped her eyes, but not until they had again sought and half-reproved the brightening eyes of Carroll.

"But," said Garnier, with a sudden change from his easy security and courteous indifference to an almost harsh impatience, "you do not mean to say, Mademoiselle, that you have the least belief in this rubbish, this ridiculous canard?"

Maruja's straight mouth quickly tightened over her teeth. She shot a significant glance at Carroll, but instantly resumed her former manner.

"It matters little what a foolish girl like myself believes. The rest of the family, even the servants and children, all believe it. It is a part of their religion. Look at these flowers around the pear-tree, and scattered on that Indian mound. They regularly find their way there on saints' days and festas. THEY are not rubbish, Monsieur Garnier; they are propitiatory sacrifices. Pereo would believe that a temblor would swallow up the casa if we should ever forego these customary rites. Is it a mere absurdity that forced my father to build these modern additions around the heart of the old adobe house, leaving it untouched, so that the curse might not be fulfilled even by implication?"

She had assumed an air of such pretty earnestness and passion; her satin face was illuminated as by some softly sensuous light within more bewildering than mere color, that Garnier, all devoted eyes and courteous blandishment, broke out: "But this curse must fall harmlessly before the incarnation of blessing; Miss Saltonstall has no more to fear than the angels. She is the one predestined through her charm, through her goodness, to lift it forever."

Carroll could not have helped echoing the aspirations of his rival, had not the next words of his mistress thrilled him with superstitious terror.

"A thousand thanks, Senor. Who knows? But I shall have warning when it falls. A day or two before the awful invader arrives, a coyote suddenly appears in broad daylight, mysteriously, near the casa. This midnight marauder, now banished to the thickest canyon, comes again to prowl around the home of his ancestors. Caramba! Senor Captain, what are you staring at? You frighten me! Stop it, I say!"

She had turned upon him, stamping her little foot in quite a frightened, childlike way.

"Nothing," laughed Carroll, the quick blood returning to his cheek. "But you must not be angry with one for being quite carried away with your dramatic intensity. By Jove! I thought I could see the WHOLE thing while you were speaking—the old Indian, the priest, and the coyote!" His eyes sparkled. The wild thought had occurred to him that perhaps, in spite of himself, he was the young woman's predestined fate; and in the very selfishness of his passion he smiled at the mere material loss of lands and prestige that would follow it. "Then the coyote has always preceded some change in the family fortunes?" he asked, boldly.

"On my mother's wedding-day," said Maruja, in a lower voice, "after the party had come from church to supper in the old casa, my father asked, 'What dog is that under the table?' When they lifted the cloth to look, a coyote rushed from the very midst of the guests and dashed out across the patio. No one knew how or when he entered."

"Heaven grant that we do not find he has eaten our breakfast!" said Garnier, gayly, "for I judge it is waiting us. I hear your sister's voice among the others crossing the lawn. Shall we tear ourselves away from the tombs of our ancestors, and join them?"

"Not as I am looking now, thank you," said Maruja, throwing the lace over her head. "I shall not submit myself to a comparison of their fresher faces and toilets by you two gentlemen. Go you both and join them. I shall wait and say an Ave for the soul of Koorotora, and slip back alone the way I came."

She had steadily evaded the pleading glance of Carroll, and though her bright face and unblemished toilet showed the inefficiency of her excuse, it was evident that her wish to be alone was genuine and without coquetry. They could only lift their hats and turn regretfully away.

As the red cap of the young officer disappeared amidst the evergreen foliage, the young woman uttered a faint sigh, which she repeated a moment after as a slight nervous yawn. Then she opened and shut her fan once or twice, striking the sticks against her little pale palm, and then, gathering the lace under her oval chin with one hand, and catching her fan and skirt with the other, bent her head and dipped into the bushes. She came out on the other side near a low fence, that separated the park from a narrow lane which communicated with the high road beyond. As she neared the fence, a slinking figure limped along the lane before her. It was the tramp of the early morning.

They raised their heads at the same moment and their eyes met. The tramp, in that clearer light, showed a spare, but bent figure, roughly clad in a miner's shirt and canvas trousers, splashed and streaked with soil, and half hidden in a ragged blue cast-off army overcoat lazily hanging from one shoulder. His thin sun-burnt face was not without a certain sullen, suspicious intelligence, and a look of half-sneering defiance. He stopped, as a startled, surly animal might have stopped at some unusual object, but did not exhibit any other discomposure. Maruja stopped at the same moment on her side of the fence.

The tramp looked at her deliberately, and then slowly lowered his eyes. "I'm looking for the San Jose road, hereabouts. Ye don't happen to know it?" he said, addressing himself to the top of the fence.

It had been said that it was not Maruja's way to encounter man, woman, or child, old or young, without an attempt at subjugation. Strong in her power and salient with fascination, she leaned gently over the fence, and with the fan raised to her delicate ear, made him repeat his question under the soft fire of her fringed eyes. He did so, but incompletely, and with querulous laziness.

"Lookin'—for—San Jose road—here'bouts."

"The road to San Jose," said Maruja, with gentle slowness, as if not unwilling to protract the conversation, "is about two miles from here. It is the high road to the left fronting the plain. There is another way, if—"

"Don't want it! Mornin'."

He dropped his head suddenly forward, and limped away in the sunlight.

CHAPTER III

Breakfast, usually a movable feast at La Mision Perdida, had been prolonged until past midday; the last of the dance guests had flown, and the home party—with the exception of Captain Carroll, who had returned to duty at his distant post —were dispersing; some as riding cavalcades to neighboring points of interest; some to visit certain notable mansions which the wealth of a rapid civilization had erected in that fertile valley. One of these in particular, the work of a breathless millionaire, was famous for the spontaneity of its growth and the reckless extravagance of its appointments.

"If you go to Aladdin's Palace," said Maruja, from the top step of the south porch, to a wagonette of guests, "after you've seen the stables with mahogany fittings for one hundred horses, ask Aladdin to show you the enchanted chamber, inlaid with California woods and paved with gold quartz."

"We would have a better chance if the Princess of China would only go with us," pleaded Garnier, gallantly.

"The Princess will stay at home with her mother, like a good girl," returned Maruja, demurely.

"A bad shot of Garnier's this time," whispered Raymond to

Buchanan, as the vehicle rolled away with them. "The Princess is not likely to visit Aladdin again."

"Why?"

"The last time she was there, Aladdin was a little too Persian in his extravagance: offered her his house, stables, and himself."

"Not a bad catch—why, he's worth two millions, I hear."

"Yes; but his wife is as extravagant as himself."

"His WIFE, eh? Ah, are you serious; or must you say something derogatory of the lassie's admirers too?" said Buchanan, playfully threatening him with his cane. "Another word, and I'll throw you from the wagon."

After their departure, the outer shell of the great house fell into a profound silence, so hollow and deserted that one might have thought the curse of Koorotora had already descended upon it. Dead leaves of roses and fallen blossoms from the long line of vine-wreathed columns lay thick on the empty stretch of brown veranda, or rustled and crept against the sides of the house, where the regular breath of the afternoon "trades" began to arise. A few cardinal flowers fell like drops of blood before the open windows of the vacant ball-room, in which the step of a solitary servant echoed faintly. It was Maruja's maid, bringing a note to her young mistress, who, in a flounced morning dress, leaned against the window. Maruja took it, glanced at it quietly, folded it in a long fold, and put it openly in her belt. Captain Carroll, from whom it came, might have carried one of his despatches as methodically. The waiting-woman noticed the act, and was moved to suggest some more exciting confidences.

"The Dona Maruja has, without doubt, noticed the bouquet on her dressing-room table from the Senor Garnier?"

The Dona Maruja had. The Dona Maruja had also learned with pain that, bribed by Judas-like coin, Faquita had betrayed the secrets of her wardrobe to the extent of furnishing a ribbon from a certain yellow dress to the Senor Buchanan to match with a Chinese fan. This was intolerable!

Faquita writhed in remorse, and averred that through this solitary act she had dishonored her family.

The Dona Maruja, however, since it was so, felt that the only thing left to do was to give her the polluted dress, and trust that the Devil might not fly away with her.

Leaving the perfectly consoled Faquita, Maruja crossed the large hall, and, opening a small door, entered a dark passage through the thick adobe wall of the old casa, and apparently left the present century behind her. A peaceful atmosphere of the past surrounded her not only in the low vaulted halls terminating in grilles or barred windows; not only in the square chambers whose dark rich but scanty furniture was only a foil to the central elegance of the lace-bordered bed and pillows; but in a certain mysterious odor of dried and desiccated religious respectability that penetrated every-where, and made the grateful twilight redolent of the generations of forgotten Guitierrez who had quietly exhaled in the old house. A mist as of incense and flowers that had lost their first bloom veiled the vista of the long corridor, and made the staring blue sky, seen through narrow windows and loopholes, glitter like mirrors let into the walls. The chamber assigned to the young ladies seemed half oratory and half sleeping-room, with a strange mingling of the convent in the bare white walls, hung only with crucifixes and religious emblems, and of the seraglio in the glimpses of lazy figures, reclining in the deshabille of short silken saya, low camisa, and dropping slippers. In a broad angle of the corridor giving upon the patio, its balustrade hung with brightly colored serapes and shawls, surrounded by voluble domestics and relations, the mistress of the casa half reclined in a hammock and gave her noonday audience.

Maruja pushed her way through the clustered stools and cushions to her mother's side, kissed her on the forehead, and then lightly perched herself like a white dove on the railing. Mrs. Saltonstall, a dark, corpulent woman, redeemed only from coarseness by a certain softness of expression and refinement of gesture, raised her heavy brown eyes to her daughter's face.

"You have not been to bed, Mara?"

"No, dear. Do I look it?"

"You must lie down presently. They tell me that Captain Carroll returned suddenly this morning."

"Do you care?"

"Who knows? Amita does not seem to fancy Jose, Esteban, Jorge, or any of her cousins. She won't look at Juan Estudillo. The Captain is not bad. He is of the government. He is—"

"Not more than ten leagues from here," said Maruja, playing with the Captain's note in her belt. "You can send for him, dear little mother. He will be glad."

"You will ever talk lightly—like your father! She was not then grieved—our Amita—eh?"

"She and Dorotea and the two Wilsons went off with Raymond and your Scotch friend in the wagonette. She did not cry—to Raymond."

"Good," said Mrs. Saltonstall, leaning back in her hammock. "Raymond is an old friend. You had better take your siesta now, child, to be bright for dinner. I expect a visitor this afternoon—Dr. West."

"Again! What will Pereo say, little mother?"

"Pereo," said the widow, sitting up again in her hammock, with impatience, "Pereo is becoming intolerable. The man is as mad as Don Quixote; it is impossible to conceal his eccentric impertinence and interference from strangers, who can not understand his confidential position in our house or his long service. There are no more mayordomos, child. The Vallejos, the Briones, the Castros, do without them now. Dr. West says, wisely, they are ridiculous survivals of the patriarchal system."

"And can be replaced by intelligent strangers," interrupted Maruja, demurely.

"The more easily if the patriarchal system has not been able to preserve the respect due from children to parents. No, Maruja! No; I am offended. Do not touch me! And your hair is coming down, and your eyes have rings like owls. You uphold this fanatical Pereo because he leaves YOU alone and stalks your poor sisters and their escorts like the Indian, whose blood is in his veins. The saints only can tell if he did not disgust this Captain Carroll into flight. He believes himself the sole custodian of the honor of our family—that he has a sacred mission from this Don Fulano of Koorotora to avert its fate. Without doubt he keeps up his delusions with aguardiente, and passes for a prophet among the silly peons and servants. He frightens the children with his ridiculous stories, and teaches them to decorate that heathen mound as if it were a shrine of Our Lady of Sorrows. He was almost rude to Dr. West yesterday."

"But you have encouraged him in his confidential position here," said Maruja. "You forget, my mother, how you got him to 'duena' Euriqueta with the Colonel Brown; how you let him frighten the young Englishman who was too attentive to Dorotea; how you set him even upon poor Raymond, and failed so dismally that I had to take him myself in hand."

"But if I choose to charge him with explanations that I can not make myself without derogating from the time-honored hospitality of the casa, that is another thing. It is not," said Dona Maria, with a certain massive dignity, that, inconsistent as it was with the weakness of her argument, was not without impressiveness, "it is not yet, Blessed Santa Maria, that we are obliged to take notice ourself of the pretensions of every guest beneath our roof like the match-making, daughter-selling English and Americans. And THEN Pereo had tact and discrimination. Now he is mad! There are strangers and strangers. The whole valley is full of them—one can discriminate, since the old families year by year are growing less."

"Surely not," said Maruja, innocently. "There is the excellent Ramierrez, who has lately almost taken him a wife from the singing-hall in San Francisco; he may yet be snatched from the fire. There is the youthful Jose Castro, the sole padrono of our national bull-fight at Soquel, the famous horse-breaker, and the winner of I know not how many races. And have we not Vincente Peralta, who will run, it is said, for the American Congress. He can read and write—truly I have a letter from him here." She turned back the folded slip of Captain Carroll's note and discovered another below.

Mrs. Saltonstall tapped her daughter's hand with her fan. "You jest at them, yet you uphold Pereo! Go, now, and sleep yourself into a better frame of mind. Stop! I hear the Doctor's horse. Run and see that Pereo receives him properly."

Maruja had barely entered the dark corridor when she came upon the visitor,—a gray, hard-featured man of sixty,—who had evidently entered without ceremony. "I see you did not wait to be announced," she said, sweetly. "My mother will be flattered by your impatience. You will find her in the patio."

"Pereo did not announce me, as he was probably still under the effect of the aguardiente he swallowed yesterday," said the Doctor, dryly. "I met him outside the tienda on the highway the other night, talking to a pair of cut-throats that I would shoot on sight."

"The mayordomo has many purchases to make, and must meet a great many people," said Maruju. "What would you? We can not select HIS acquaintances; we can hardly choose our own," she added, sweetly.

The Doctor hesitated, as if to reply, and then, with a grim "Good-morning," passed on towards the patio. Maruja did not follow him. Her attention was suddenly absorbed by a hitherto unnoticed motionless figure, that seemed to be hiding in the shadow of an angle of the passage, as if waiting for her to pass. The keen eyes of the daughter of Joseph Saltonstall were not deceived. She walked directly towards the figure, and said, sharply, "Pereo!"

The figure came hesitatingly forward into the light of the grated window. It was that of an old man, still tall and erect, though the hair had disappeared from his temples, and hung in two or three straight, long dark elf-locks on his neck. His face, over which one of the bars threw a sinister shadow, was the yellow of a dried tobacco-leaf, and veined as strongly. His garb was a strange mingling of the vaquero and the ecclesiastic—velvet trousers, open from the knee down, and fringed with bullion buttons; a broad red sash around his waist, partly hidden by a long, straight chaqueta; with a circular sacerdotal cape of black broadcloth slipped over his head through a slit-like opening braided with gold. His restless yellow eyes fell before the young girl's; and the stiff, varnished, hard-brimmed sombrero he held in his wrinkled hands trembled.

"You are spying again, Pereo," said Maruja, in another dialect than the one she had used to her mother. "It is unworthy of my father's trusted servant."

"It is that man—that coyote, Dona Maruja, that is unworthy of your father, of your mother, of YOU!" he gesticulated, in a fierce whisper. "I, Pereo, do not spy. I follow, follow the track of the prowling, stealing brute until I run him down. Yes, it was I, Pereo, who warned your father he would not be content with the half of the land he stole! It was I, Pereo, who warned your mother that each time he trod the soil of La Mision Perdida he measured the land he could take away!" He stopped pantingly, with the insane abstraction of a fixed idea glittering in his eyes.

"And it was YOU, Pereo," she said, caressingly, laying her soft hand on his heaving breast, "YOU who carried me in your arms when I was a child. It was you, Pereo, who took me before you on your pinto horse to the rodeo, when no one knew it but ourselves, my Pereo, was it not?" He nodded his head violently. "It was you who showed me the gallant caballeros, the Pachecos, the Castros, the Alvarados, the Estudillos, the Peraltas, the Vallejos." His head kept time with each name as the fire dimmed in his wet eyes. "You made me promise I would not forget them for the

Americanos who were here. Good! That was years ago! I am older now. I have seen many Americans. Well, I am still free!"

He caught her hand, and raised it to his lips with a gesture almost devotional. His eyes softened; as the exaltation of passion passed, his voice dropped into the querulousness of privileged age. "Ah, yes!—you, the first-born, the heiress—of a verity, yes! You were ever a Guitierrez. But the others? Eh, where are they now? And it was always: 'Eh, Pereo, what shall we do to-day? Pereo, good Pereo, we are asked to ride here and there; we are expected to visit the new people in the valley—what say you, Pereo? Who shall we dine to-day?' Or: 'Enquire me of this or that strange caballero—and if we may speak.' Ah, it is but yesterday that Amita would say: 'Lend me thine own horse, Pereo, that I may outstrip this swaggering Americano that clings ever to my side,' ha! ha! Or the grave Dorotea would whisper: 'Convey to this Senor Presumptuous Pomposo that the daughters of Guitierrez do not ride alone with strangers!' Or even the little Liseta would say, he! he! 'Why does the stranger press my foot in his great hand when he helps me into the saddle? Tell him that is not the way, Pereo.' Ha! ha!" He laughed childishly, and stopped. "And why does Senorita Amita now—look—complain that Pereo, old Pereo, comes between her and this Senor Raymond—this maquinista? Eh, and why does SHE, the lady mother, the Castellana, shut Pereo from her councils?" he went on, with rising excitement. "What are these secret meetings, eh?—what these appointments, alone with this Judas—without the family—without ME!"

"Hearken, Pereo," said the young girl, again laying her hand on the old man's shoulder; "you have spoken truly—but you forget—the years pass. These are no longer strangers; old friends have gone—these have taken their place. My father forgave the Doctor—why can not you? For the rest, believe in me—me—Maruja"—she dramatically touched her heart over the international complications of the letters of Captain Carroll and Peralta. "I will see that the family honor does not suffer. And now, good Pereo, calm thyself. Not with aguardiente, but with a bottle of old wine from the Mision refectory that I will send to thee. It was given to me by thy friend, Padre Miguel, and is from the old vines that were here. Courage, Pereo! And thou sayest that Amita complains that thou comest between her and Raymond. So! What matter? Let it cheer thy heart to know that I have summoned the Peraltas, the Pachecos, the Estudillos, all thy old friends, to dine here to-day. Thou wilt hear the old names, even if the faces are young to thee. Courage! Do thy duty, old friend; let them see that the hospitality of La Mision Perdida does not grow old, if its mayordomo does. Faquita will bring thee the wine. No; not that way; thou needest not pass the patio, nor meet that man again. Here, give me thy hand. I will lead thee. It trembles, Pereo! These are not the sinews that only two years ago pulled down the bull at Soquel with thy single lasso! Why, look! I can drag thee; see!" and with a light laugh and a boyish gesture, she half pulled, half dragged him along, until their voices were lost in the dark corridor.

Maruja kept her word. When the sun began to cast long shadows along the veranda, not only the outer shell of La Mision Perdida, but the dark inner heart of the old casa, stirred with awakened life. Single horsemen and carriages began to arrive; and, mingled with the modern turnouts of the home party and the neighboring Americans, were a few of the cumbrous vehicles and chariots of fifty years ago, drawn by gayly trapped mules with bizarre postilions, and occasionally an outrider. Dark faces looked from the balcony of the patio, a light cloud of cigarette-smoke made the dark corridors the more obscure, and mingled with the forgotten incense. Bare-headed pretty women, with roses starring their dark hair, wandered with childish curiosity along the broad veranda and in and out of the French windows that opened upon the grand saloon. Scrupulously shaved men with olive complexion, stout men with accurately curving whiskers meeting at their dimpled chins, lounged about with a certain unconscious dignity that made them contentedly indifferent to any novelty of their surroundings. For a while the two races kept mechanically apart; but, through the tactful gallantry of Garnier, the cynical familiarity of Raymond, and the impulsive recklessness of Aladdin, who had forsaken his enchanted Palace on the slightest of invitations, and returned with the party in the hope of again seeing the Princess of China, an interchange of civilities, of gallantries, and even of confidences, at last took place. Jovita Castro had heard (who had not?) of the wonders of Aladdin's Palace, and was it of actual truth that the ladies had a bouquet and a fan to match their dress presented to them every morning, and that the gentlemen had a champagne cocktail sent to their rooms before breakfast? "Just you come, Miss, and bring your father and your brothers, and stay a week and you'll see," responded Aladdin, gallantly. "Hold on! What's your father's first name? I'll send a team over there for you to-morrow." "And is it true that you frightened the handsome Captain Carroll away from Amita?" said Dolores Briones, over the edge of her fan to Raymond. "Perfectly," said Raymond, with ingenuous frankness. "I made it a matter of life or death. He was a soldier, and naturally preferred the former as giving him a better chance for promotion." "Ah! we thought it was Maruja you liked best." "That was two years ago," said Raymond, gravely. "And you Americanos can change in that time?" "I have just experienced that it can be done in less," he responded, over the fan, with bewildering significance. Nor were these confidences confined to only one nationality. "I always thought you Spanish gentlemen were very dark, and wore long mustaches and a cloak," said pretty little Miss Walker, gazing frankly into the smooth round face of the eldest Pacheco—"why, you are as fair as I am," "Eaf I tink that, I am for ever mizzarable," he replied, with grave melancholy. In the dead silence that followed he was enabled to make his decorous point. "Because I shall not ezeape ze fate of Narcissus." Mr. Buchanan, with the unrestrained and irresponsible enjoyment of a traveler, entered fully into the spirit of the scene. He even found words of praise for Aladdin, whose extravagance had at first seemed to him almost impious. "Eh, but I'm not prepared to say he is a fool, either," he remarked to his friend the San Francisco banker. "Those who try to pick him up for one," returned the banker, "will find themselves mistaken. His is the prodigality that loosens others' purse-strings besides his own, Everybody contents himself with criticising his way of spending money, but is ready to follow his way of making it."

The dinner was more formal, and when the mistress of the house, massive in black silk, velvet and gold embroidery, moved like a pageant to the head of her table, where she remained like a sacerdotal effigy, not even the presence of the practical Scotchman at her side could remove the prevailing sense of restraint. For a while the conversation of the relatives might have been brought with them in their antique vehicles of fifty years ago, so faded, so worn, and so springless it was. General Pico related the festivities at Monterey, on the occasion of the visit of Sir George Simpson early in the present century, of which he was an eyewitness, with great precision of detail. Don Juan Estudillo was comparatively frivolous, with anecdotes of Louis Philippe, whom he had seen in Paris. Far-seeing Pedro Guitierrez was gloomily impressed with a Mongolian invasion of California by the Chinese, in which the prevailing religion would be supplanted by heathen temples, and polygamy engrafted on the Constitution. Everybody agreed however, that the vital question of the hour was the settlement of land titles— Americans who claimed under preemption and the native holders of Spanish grants were equally of the opinion.

In the midst of this the musical voice of Maruja was heard saying, "What is a tramp?"

Raymond, on her right, was ready but not conclusive.

A tramp, if he could sing, would be a troubadour; if he could pray, would be a pilgrim friar—in either case a natural object of womanly solicitude. But as he could do neither, he was simply a curse.

"And you think that is not an object of womanly solicitude? But that does not tell me WHAT he is."

A dozen gentlemen, swept in the radius of those softly-inquiring eyes, here started to explain. From them it appeared that there was no such thing in California as a tramp, and there were also a dozen varieties of tramp in California.

"But is he always very uncivil?" asked Maruja.

Again there were conflicting opinions. You might have to shoot him on sight, and you might have him invariably run from you. When the question was finally settled, Maruja was found to have become absorbed in conversation with some one else.

Amita, a taller copy of Maruja, and more regularly beautiful, had built up a little pile of bread crumbs between herself and Raymond, and was listening to him with a certain shy, girlish interest that was as inconsistent with the serene regularity of her face as Maruja's self-possessed, subtle intelligence was incongruous to her youthful figure. Raymond's voice, when he addressed Amita, was low and earnest; not from any significance of matter, but from its frank confidential quality.

"They are discussing the new railroad project, and your relations are all opposed to it; to-morrow they will each apply privately to Aladdin for the privilege of subscribing."

"I have never seen a railroad," said Amita, slightly coloring; "but you are an engineer, and I know they must be some thing very clever."

Notwithstanding the coolness of the night, a full moon drew the guests to the veranda, where coffee was served, and where, mysteriously muffled in cloaks and shawls, the party took upon itself the appearance of groups of dominoed masqueraders, scattered along the veranda and on the broad steps of the porch in gypsy-like encampments, from whose cloaked shadow the moonlight occasionally glittered upon a varnished boot or peeping satin slipper. Two or three of these groups had resolved themselves into detached couples, who wandered down the acacia walk to the sound of a harp in the grand saloon or the occasional uplifting of a thin Spanish tenor. Two of these couples were Maruja and Garnier, followed by Amita and Raymond.

"You are restless to-night, Maruja," said Amita, shyly endeavoring to make a show of keeping up with her sister's boyish stride, in spite of Raymond's reluctance. "You are paying for your wakefulness to-day."

The same idea passed through the minds of both men. She was missing the excitement of Captain Carroll's presence.

"The air is so refreshing away from the house," responded Maruja, with a bright energy that belied any suggestion of fatigue or moral disquietude. "I'm tired of running against those turtle-doves in the walks and bushes. Let us keep on to the lane. If you are tired, Mr. Raymond will give you his arm."

They kept on, led by the indomitable little figure, who, for once, did not seem to linger over the attentions, both piquant and tender, with which Garnier improved his opportunity. Given a shadowy lane, a lovers' moon, a pair of bright and not unkindly eyes, a charming and not distant figure—what more could he want? Yet he wished she hadn't walked so fast. One might be vivacious, audacious, brilliant, at an Indian trot; but impassioned—never! The pace increased; they were actually hurrying. More than that, Maruja had struck into a little trot; her lithe body swaying from side to side, her little feet straight as an arrow before her; accompanying herself with a quaint musical chant, which she obligingly explained had been taught her as a child by Pereo. They stopped only at the hedge, where she had that morning encountered the tramp.

There is little doubt that the rest of the party was disconcerted: Amita, whose figure was not adapted to this Camilla-like exercise; Raymond, who was annoyed at the poor girl's discomfiture; and Garnier, who had lost a golden opportunity, with the faint suspicion of having looked ridiculous. Only Maruja's eyes, or rather the eyes of her lamented father, seemed to enjoy it.

"You are too effeminate," she said, leaning against the fence, and shading her eyes with her fan, as she glanced around in the staring moonlight. "Civilization has taken away your legs. A man ought to be able to trust to his feet all day, and to nothing else."

"In fact—a tramp," suggested Raymond.

"Possibly. I think I should like to have been a gypsy, and to have wandered about, finding a new home every night."

"And a change of linen on the early morning hedges," said

Raymond. "But do you think seriously that you and your sister are suitably clad to commence to-night. It is bitterly cold," he added, turning up his collar. "Could you begin by showing a pal the nearest haystack or hen-roost?"

"Sybarite!" She cast a long look over the fields and down the lane. Suddenly she started. "What is that?"

She pointed to a tall erect figure slowly disappearing on the other side of the hedge.

"It's Pereo, only Pereo. I knew him by his long serape," said Garnier, who was nearest the hedge, complacently. "But what is surprising, he was not there when we came, nor did he come out of that open field. He must have been walking behind us on the other side of the hedge."

The eyes of the two girls sought each other simultaneously, but not without Raymond's observant glance. Amita's brow darkened as she moved to her sister's side, and took her arm with a confidential pressure that was returned. The two men, with a vague consciousness of some contretemps, dropped a pace behind, and began to talk to each other, leaving the sisters to exchange a few words in a low tone as they slowly returned to the house.

Meanwhile, Pereo's tall figure had disappeared in the shrubbery, to emerge again in the open area by the summer-house and the old pear-tree. The red sparks of two or three cigarettes in the shadow of the summer-house, and the crouching forms of two shawled women came forward to greet him.

"And what hast thou heard, Pereo?" said one of the women.

"Nothing," said Pereo, impatiently. "I told thee I would

answer for this little primogenita with my life. She is but leading this Frenchman a dance, as she has led the others, and the Dona Amita and her Raymond are but wax in her hands. Besides, I have spoken with the little 'Ruja to-day, and spoke my mind, Pepita, and she says there is nothing."

"And whilst thou wert speaking to her, my poor Pereo, the devil of an American Doctor was speaking to her mother, thy mistress—our mistress, Pereo! Wouldst thou know what he said? Oh, it was nothing."

"Now, the curse of Koorotora on thee, Pepita!" said Pereo, excitedly. "Speak, fool, if thou knowest anything!"

"Of a verity, no. Let Faquita, then, speak: she heard it." She reached out her hand, and dragged Maruja's maid, not unwilling, before the old man.

"Good! 'Tis Faquita, daughter of Gomez, and a child of the land. Speak, little one. What said this coyote to the mother of thy mistress?"

"Truly, good Pereo, it was but accident that befriended me."

"Truly, for thy mistress's sake, I hoped it had been more. But let that go. Come, what said he, child?"

"I was hanging up a robe behind the curtain in the oratory when Pepita ushered in the Americano. I had no time to fly."

"Why shouldst thou fly from a dog like this?" said one of the cigarette-smokers who had drawn near.

"Peace!" said the old man.

"When the Dona Maria joined him they spoke of affairs.

Yes, Pereo, she, thy mistress, spoke of affairs to this man—ay, as she might have talked to THEE. And, could he advise this? and could he counsel that? and should the cattle be taken from the lower lands, and the fields turned to grain? and had he a purchaser for Los Osos?"

"Los Osos! It is the boundary land—the frontier—the line of the arroyo—older than the Mision," muttered Pereo.

"Ay, and he talked of the—the—I know not what it is!—the r-r-rail-r-road."

"The railroad," gasped the old man. "I will tell thee what it is! It is the cut of a burning knife through La Mision Perdida—as long as eternity, as dividing as death. On either side of that gash life is blasted; wherever that cruel steel is laid the track of it is livid and barren; it cuts down all barriers; leaps all boundaries, be they canada or canyon; it is a torrent in the plain, a tornado in the forest; its very pathway is destruction to whoso crosses it—man or beast; it is the heathenish God of the Americanos; they build temples for it, and flock there and worship it whenever it stops, breathing fire and flame like a very Moloch."

"Eh! St. Anthony preserve us!" said Faquita, shuddering; "and yet they spoke of it as 'shares' and 'stocks,' and said it would double the price of corn."

"Now, Judas pursue thee and thy railroad, Pereo," said Pepita, impatiently. "It is not such bagatela that Faquita is here to relate. Go on, child, and tell all that happened."

"And then," continued Faquita, with a slight affectation of maiden bashfulness, in the closer-drawing circle of cigarettes, "and then they talked of other things and of themselves; and, of a verity, this gray-bearded Doctor will play the goat and utter gallant speeches, and speak of a lifelong devotion and of the time he should have a right to protect—"

"The right, girl! Didst thou say the right? No, thou didst mistake. It was not THAT he meant?"

"Thy life to a quarter peso that the little Faquita does not mistake," said the evident satirist of the household. "Trust to Gomez' muchacha to understand a proposal."

When the laugh was over, and the sparks of the cigarette, cleverly whipped out of the speaker's lips by Faquita's fan, had disappeared in the darkness, she resumed, pettishly, "I know not what you call it when he kissed her hand and held it to his heart."

"Judas!" gasped Pereo. "But," he added, feverishly, "she, the Dona Maria, thy mistress, SHE summoned thee at once to call me to cast out this dust into the open air; thou didst fly to her assistance? What! thou sawest this, and did nothing— eh?" He stopped, and tried to peer into the girl's face. "No! Ah, I see; I am an old fool. Yes; it was Maruja's own mother that stood there. He! he! he!" he laughed piteously; "and she smiled and smiled and broke the coward's heart, as Maruja might. And when he was gone, she bade thee bring her water to wash the filthy Judas stain from her hand."

"Santa Ana!" said Faquita, shrugging her shoulders. "She did what the veriest muchacha would have done. When he had gone, she sat down and cried."

The old man drew back a step, and steadied himself by the table. Then, with a certain tremulous audacity, he began: "So! that is all you have to tell—nothing! Bah! A lazy slut sleeps at her duty, and dreams behind a curtain! Yes, dreams!—you understand—dreams! And for this she leaves her occupations, and comes to gossip here! Come," he continued, steadily working himself into a passion, "come, enough of this! Get you gone!—you, and Pepita, and Andreas, and Victor—all of you—back to your duty. Away! Am I not master here? Off! I say!"

There was no mistaking the rising anger of his voice. The cowed group rose in a frightened way and disappeared one by one silently through the labyrinth. Pereo waited until the last had vanished, and then, cramming his stiff sombrero over his eyes with an ejaculation, brushed his way through the shrubbery in the direction of the stables.

Later, when the full glory of the midnight moon had put out every straggling light in the great house; when the long veranda slept in massive bars of shadow, and even the tradewinds were hushed to repose, Pereo silently issued from the stable-yard in vaquero's dress, mounted and caparisoned. Picking his way cautiously along the turf-bordered edge of the gravel path, he noiselessly reached a gate that led to the lane. Walking his spirited mustang with difficulty until the house had at last disappeared in the intervening foliage, he turned with an easy canter into a border bridle-path that seemed to lead to the canada. In a quarter of an hour he had reached a low amphitheatre of meadows, shut in a half circle of grassy treeless hills.

Here, putting spurs to his horse, he entered upon a singular exercise. Twice he made a circuit of the meadow at a wild gallop, with flying serape and loosened rein, and twice returned. The third time his speed increased; the ground seemed to stream from under him; in the distance the limbs of his steed became invisible in their furious action, and, lying low forward on his mustang's neck, man and horse passed like an arrowy bolt around the circle. Then something like a light ring of smoke up-curved from the saddle before him, and, slowly uncoiling itself in mid air, dropped gently to the ground as he passed. Again, and once again, the shadowy coil sped upward and onward, slowly detaching its snaky rings with a weird deliberation that was in strange contrast to the impetuous onset of the rider, and yet seemed a part of his fury. And then turning, Pereo trotted gently to the centre of the circle.

Here he divested himself of his serape, and, securing it in a cylindrical roll, placed it upright on the ground and once more sped away on his furious circuit. But this time he wheeled suddenly before it was half completed and bore down directly upon the unconscious object. Within a hundred feet he swerved slightly; the long detaching rings again writhed in mid air and softly descended as he thundered past. But when he had reached the line of circuit again, he turned and made directly for the road he had entered. Fifty feet behind his horse's heels, at the end of a shadowy cord, the luckless serape was dragging and bounding after him!

"The old man is quiet enough this morning," said Andreas, as he groomed the sweat-dried skin of the mustang the next day. "It is easy to see, friend Pinto, that he has worked off his madness on thee."

CHAPTER IV

The Rancho of San Antonio might have been a characteristic asylum for its blessed patron, offering as it did a secure retreat from temptations for the carnal eye, and affording every facility for uninterrupted contemplation of the sky above, unbroken by tree or elevation. Unlike La Mision Perdida, of which it had been part, it was a level plain of rich adobe, half the year presenting a billowy sea of tossing verdure breaking on the far-off horizon line, half the year presenting a dry and dusty shore, from which the vernal sea had ebbed, to the low sky that seemed to mock it with a visionary sea beyond. A row of rough, irregular, and severely practical sheds and buildings housed the machinery and the fifty or sixty men employed in the cultivation of the soil, but neither residential mansion nor farmhouse offered any nucleus of rural comfort or civilization in the midst of this wild expanse of earth and sky. The simplest adjuncts of country life were unknown: milk and butter were brought from the nearest town; weekly supplies of fresh meat and vegetables came from the same place; in the harvest season, the laborers and harvesters lodged and boarded in the adjacent settlement and walked to their work. No cultivated flower bloomed beside the unpainted tenement, though the fields were starred in early spring with poppies and daisies; the humblest garden plant or herb had no place in that prolific soil. The serried ranks of wheat pressed closely round the straggling sheds and barns and hid the lower windows. But the sheds were fitted with the latest agricultural machinery; a telegraphic wire connected the nearest town with an office in the wing of one of the buildings, where Dr. West sat, and in the midst of the wilderness severely checked his accounts with nature.

Whether this strict economy of domestic outlay arose from an ostentatious contempt of country life and the luxurious habits of the former landholders, or whether it was a purely business principle of Dr. West, did not appear. Those who knew him best declared that it was both. Certain it was that unqualified commercial success crowned and dignified his method. A few survivors of the old native families came to see his strange machinery, that did the work of so many idle men and horses. It is said that he offered to "run" the distant estate of Joaquin Padilla from his little office amidst the grain of San Antonio. Some shook their heads, and declared that he only sucked the juices of the land for a few brief years to throw it away again; that in his fierce haste he skimmed the fatness of ages of gentle cultivation on a soil that had been barely tickled with native oaken plowshares.

His own personal tastes and habits were as severe and practical as his business: the little wing he inhabited contained only his office, his living room or library, his bedroom, and a bath-room. This last inconsistent luxury was due to a certain cat-like cleanliness which was part of his nature. His iron-gray hair—a novelty in this country of young Americans—was always scrupulously brushed, and his linen spotless. A slightly professional and somewhat old-fashioned respectability in his black clothes was also characteristic. His one concession to the customs of his neighbors was the possession of two or three of the half-broken and spirited mustangs of the country, which he rode with the fearlessness, if not the perfect security and ease, of a native. Whether the subjection of this lawless and powerful survival of a wild and unfettered nature around him was part of his plan, or whether it was only a lingering trait of some younger prowess, no one knew; but his grim and decorous figure, contrasting with the picturesque and flowing freedom of the horse he bestrode, was a frequent spectacle in road and field.

It was the second day after his visit to La Mision Perdida. He was sitting by his desk, at sunset, in the faint afterglow of the western sky, which flooded the floor through the open door. He was writing, but presently lifted his head, with an impatient air, and called out, "Harrison!"

The shadow of Dr. West's foreman appeared at the door.

"Who's that you're talking to?"

"Tramp, Sir."

"Hire him, or send him about his business. Don't stand gabbling there."

"That's just it, sir. He won't hire for a week or a day. He says he'll do an odd job for his supper and a shakedown, but no more."

"Pack him off! . . . Stay. . . . What's he like?"

"Like the rest of 'em, only a little lazier, I reckon."

"Umph! Fetch him in."

The foreman disappeared, and returned with the tramp already known to the reader. He was a little dirtier and grimier than on the morning he had addressed Maruja at La

Mision Perdida; but he wore the same air of sullen indifference, occasionally broken by furtive observation. His laziness—or weariness—if the term could describe the lassitude of perfect physical condition, seemed to have increased; and he leaned against the door as the Doctor regarded him with slow contempt. The silence continuing, he deliberately allowed himself to slip down into a sitting position in the doorway, where he remained.

"You seem to have been born tired," said the Doctor, grimly.

"Yes."

"What have you got to say for yourself?"

"I told HIM," said the tramp, nodding his head towards the foreman, "what I'd do for a supper and a bed. I don't want anything but that."

"And if you don't get what you want on your own conditions, what'll you do?" asked the Doctor, dryly.

"Go."

"Where did you come from?"

"States."

"Where are you going?"

"On."

"Leave him to me," said Dr. West to his foreman. The man smiled, and withdrew.

The Doctor bent his head again over his accounts. The

Bret Harte

tramp, sitting in the doorway, reached out his hand, pulled a young wheat-stalk that had sprung up near the doorstep, and slowly nibbled it. He did not raise his eyes to the Doctor, but sat, a familiar culprit awaiting sentence, without fear, without hope, yet not without a certain philosophical endurance of the situation.

"Go into that passage," said the Doctor, lifting his head as he turned a page of his ledger, "and on the shelf you'll find some clothing stores for the men. Pick out something to fit you."

The tramp arose, moved towards the passage, and stopped. "It's for the job only, you understand?" he said.

"For the job," answered the Doctor.

The tramp returned in a few moments with overalls and woolen shirt hanging on his arm and a pair of boots and socks in his hand. The Doctor had put aside his pen. "Now go into that room and change. Stop! First wash the dust from your feet in that bath-room."

The tramp obeyed, and entered the room. The Doctor walked to the door, and looked out reflectively on the paling sky. When he turned again he noticed that the door of the bath-room was opened, and the tramp, who had changed his clothes by the fading light, was drying his feet. The Doctor approached, and stood for a moment watching him.

"What's the matter with your foot?"* he asked, after a pause.

* This apparent classical plagiarism is actually a fact of identification on record in the California Law Reports. It is therefore unnecessary for me to add that the attendant circumstances and characters are purely fictitious.—B. H.

"Born so."

The first and second toe were joined by a thin membrane.

"Both alike?" asked the Doctor.

"Yes," said the young man, exhibiting the other foot.

"What did you say your name was?"

"I didn't say it. It's Henry Guest, same as my father's."

"Where were you born?"

"Dentville, Pike County, Missouri."

"What was your mother's name?"

"Spalding, I reckon."

"Where are your parents now?"

"Mother got divorced from father, and married again down South, somewhere. Father left home twenty years ago. He's somewhere in California—if he ain't dead."

"He isn't dead."

"How do you know?"

"Because I am Henry Guest, of Dentville, and"—he stopped, and, shading his eyes with his hand as he deliberately examined the tramp, added coldly—"your father, I reckon."

There was a slight pause. The young man put down the boot he had taken up. "Then I'm to stay here?"

"Certainly not. Here my name is only West, and I have no son. You'll go on to San Jose, and stay there until I look into this thing. You haven't got any money, of course?" he asked, with a scarcely suppressed sneer.

"I've got a little," returned the young man.

"How much?"

The tramp put his hand into his breast, and drew out a piece of folded paper containing a single gold coin.

"Five dollars. I've kept it a month; it doesn't cost much to live as I do," he added, dryly.

"There's fifty more. Go to some hotel in San Jose, and let me know where you are. You've got to live, and you don't want to work. Well, you don't seem to be a fool; so I needn't tell you that if you expect anything from me, you must leave this matter in my hands. I have chosen to acknowledge you to-day of my own free will: I can as easily denounce you as an impostor to-morrow, if I choose. Have you told your story to any one in the valley?"

"No."

"See that you don't, then. Before you go, you must answer me a few more questions."

He drew a chair to his table, and dipped a pen in the ink, as if to take down the answers. The young man, finding the only chair thus occupied, moved the Doctor's books aside, and sat down on the table beside him.

The questions were repetitions of those already asked, but more in detail, and thoroughly practical in their nature. The answers were given straightforwardly and unconcernedly, as if the subject was not worth the trouble of invention or evasion. It was difficult to say whether questioner or answerer took least pleasure in the interrogation, which might have referred to the concerns of a third party. Both, however, spoke disrespectfully of their common family, with almost an approach to sympathetic interest.

"You might as well be going now," said the Doctor, finally rising. "You can stop at the fonda, about two miles further on, and get your supper and bed, if you like."

The young man slipped from the table, and lounged to the door. The Doctor put his hands in his pockets and followed him. The young man, as if in unconscious imitation, had put HIS hands in his pockets also, and looked at him.

"I'll hear from you, then, when you are in San Jose?" said Dr. West, looking past him into the grain, with a slight approach to constraint in his indifference.

"Yes—if that's agreed upon," returned the young man, pausing on the threshold. A faint sense of some purely conventional responsibility in their position affected them both. They would have shaken hands if either had offered the initiative. A sullen consciousness of gratuitous rectitude in the selfish mind of the father; an equally sullen conviction of twenty years of wrong in the son, withheld them both. Unpleasantly observant of each other's awkwardness, they parted with a feeling of relief.

Dr. West closed the door, lit his lamp, and, going to his desk, folded the paper containing the memoranda he had just written and placed it in his pocket. Then he summoned his foreman. The man entered, and glanced around the room as if expecting to see the Doctor's guest still there.

"Tell one of the men to bring round 'Buckeye.'"

The foreman hesitated. "Going to ride to-night, sir?"

"Certainly; I may go as far as Saltonstall's. If I do, you needn't expect me back till morning."

"Buckeye's mighty fresh to-night, boss. Regularly bucked his saddle clean off an hour ago, and there ain't a man dare exercise him."

"I'll bet he don't buck his saddle off with me on it," said the Doctor, grimly. "Bring him along."

The man turned to go. "You found the tramp pow'ful lazy, didn't ye?"

"I found a heap more in him than in some that call themselves smart," said Dr. West, unconsciously setting up an irritable defense of the absent one. "Hurry up that horse!"

The foreman vanished. The Doctor put on a pair of leather leggings, large silver spurs, and a broad soft-brimmed hat, but made no other change in his usual half-professional conventional garb. He then went to the window and glanced in the direction of the highway. Now that his son was gone, he felt a faint regret that he had not prolonged the interview. Certain peculiarities in his manner, certain suggestions of expression in his face, speech, and gesture, came back to him now with unsatisfied curiosity. "No matter," he said to himself; "he'll turn up soon again—as soon as I want him, if not sooner. He thinks he's got a mighty soft thing here, and he isn't going to let it go. And there's that same d—d sullen dirty pride of his mother, for all he doesn't cotton to her. Wonder I didn't recognize it at first. And hoarding up that five dollars! That's Jane's brat, all over! And, of course," he added, bitterly, "nothing of ME in him. No; nothing! Well, well, what's the difference?" He turned towards the door, with a certain sullen defiance in his face so like the man he believed he did not resemble, that his foreman, coming upon him suddenly, might have been startled at the likeness. Fortunately, however, Harrison was too much engrossed with the antics of the irrepressible Buckeye, which the ostler had just brought to the door, to notice anything else. The arrival of the horse changed the Doctor's expression to one of more practical and significant resistance. With the assistance of two men at the head of the restive brute, he managed to vault into the saddle. A few wild plunges only seemed to settle him the firmer in his seat—each plunge leaving its record in a thin red line on the animal's flanks, made by the cruel spurs of its rider. Any lingering desire of following his son's footsteps was quickly dissipated by Buckeye, who promptly bolted in the opposite direction, and, before Dr. West could gain active control over him, they were half a mile on their way to La Mision Perdida.

Dr. West did not regret it. Twenty years ago he had voluntarily abandoned a legal union of mutual unfaithfulness and misconduct, and allowed his wife to get the divorce he might have obtained for equal cause. He had abandoned to her the issue of that union—an infant son. Whatever he chose to do now was purely gratuitous; the only hold which this young stranger had on his respect was that HE also recognized that fact with a cold indifference equal to his own. At present the half-savage brute he bestrode occupied all his attention. Yet he could not help feeling his advancing years tell upon him more heavily that evening; fearless as he was, his strength was no longer equal when measured with the untiring youthful malevolence of his unbroken mustang. For a moment he dwelt regretfully on the lazy half-developed sinews of his son; for a briefer instant there flashed across him the thought that those sinews ought to replace his own; ought to be HIS to lean upon—that thus, and thus only, could he achieve the old miracle of restoring his lost youth by perpetuating his own power in his own blood; and he, whose profound belief in personality had rejected all hereditary principle, felt this with a sudden exquisite pain. But his horse, perhaps recognizing a relaxing grip, took that opportunity to "buck." Curving his back like a cat, and throwing himself into the air with an unexpected bound, he came down with four stiff, inflexible legs, and a shock that might have burst the saddle-girths, had not the wily old man as quickly brought the long rowels of his spurs together and fairly locked his heels under Buckeye's collapsing barrel. It was the mustang's last rebellions struggle. The discomfited brute gave in, and darted meekly and apologetically forward, and, as it were, left all its rider's doubts and fears far behind in the vanishing distance.

CHAPTER V

Meanwhile, the subject of Dr. West's meditations was slowly making his way along the high-road towards the fonda. He walked more erect and with less of a shuffle in his gait; but whether this was owing to his having cast the old skin of garments adapted to his slouch, and because he was more securely shod, or whether it was from the sudden straightening of some warped moral quality, it would have been difficult to say. The expression of his face certainly gave no evidence of actual and prospective good fortune; if anything, the lines of discontent around his brow and mouth were more strongly drawn. Apparently, his interview with his father had only the effect of reviving and stirring into greater activity a certain dogged sentiment that, through long years, had become languidly mechanical. He was no longer a beaten animal, but one roused by a chance success into a dangerous knowledge of his power. In his honest workman's dress, he was infinitely more to be feared than in his rags; in the lifting of his downcast eye, there was the revelation of a baleful intelligence. In his changed condition, civilization only seemed to have armed him against itself.

The fonda, a long low building, with a red-tiled roof extending over a porch or whitewashed veranda, in which drunken vaqueros had been known to occasionally disport their mustangs, did not offer a very reputable appearance to the eye of young Guest as he approached it in the gathering shadows. One or two half-broken horses were securely fastened to the stout cross-beams of some heavy posts driven in the roadway before it, and a primitive trough of roughly excavated stone stood near it. Through a broken gate at the side there was a glimpse of a grass-grown and deserted court-yard piled with the disused packing-cases and barrels of the tienda, or general country shop, which huddled under the same roof at the other end of the building. The opened door of the fonda showed a low-studded room fitted up with a rude imitation of an American bar on one side, and containing a few small tables, at which half a dozen men were smoking, drinking, and playing cards. The faded pictorial poster of the last bull-fight at Monterey, and an American "Sheriff's notice" were hung on the wall and in the door-way. A thick yellow atmosphere of cigarette smoke, through which the inmates appeared like brown shadows, pervaded the room.

The young man hesitated before this pestilential interior, and took a seat on a bench on the veranda. After a moment's interval, the yellow landlord came to the door with a look of inquiry, which Guest answered by a demand for lodging and supper. When the landlord had vanished again in the cigarette fog, the several other guests, one after the other, appeared at the doorway, with their cigarettes in their mouths and their cards still in their hands, and gazed upon him.

There may have been some excuse for their curiosity. As before hinted, Guest's appearance in his overalls and woolen shirt was somewhat incongruous, and, for some inexplicable reason, the same face and figure which did not look inconsistent in rags and extreme poverty now at once suggested a higher social rank both of intellect and refinement than his workman's dress indicated. This, added to his surliness of manner and expression, strengthened a growing suspicion in the mind of the party that he was a fugitive from justice—a forger, a derelict banker, or possibly a murderer. It is only fair to say that the moral sense of the spectators was not shocked at the suspicion, and that a more active sympathy was only withheld by his reticence. An unfortunate incident seemed to complete the evidence against him. In impatiently responding to the landlord's curt demand for prepayment of his supper, he allowed three or four pieces of gold to escape from his pocket on the veranda. In the quick glances of the party, as he stooped to pick them up, he read the danger of his carelessness.

His sullen self-possession did not seem to be shaken. Calling to the keeper of the tienda, who had appeared at his door in time to witness the Danae-like shower, he bade him approach, in English.

"What sort of knives have you got?"

"Knives, Senor?"

"Yes; bowie-knives or dirks. Knives like that," he said, making an imaginary downward stroke at the table before him.

The shopkeeper entered the tienda, and presently reappeared with three or four dirks in red leather sheaths. Guest selected the heaviest, and tried its point on the table.

"How much?"

"Tres pesos."

The young man threw him one of his gold pieces, and slipped the knife and its sheath in his boot. When he had received his change from the shopkeeper, he folded his arms and leaned back against the wall in quiet indifference.

The simple act seemed to check aggressive, but not insinuating, interference. In a few moments one of the men appeared at the doorway.

"It is fine weather for the road, little comrade!"

Guest did not reply.

"Ah! the night, it ess splendid," he repeated, in broken English, rubbing his hands, as if washing in the air.

Still no reply.

"You shall come from Sank Hosay?"

"I sha'ant."

The stranger muttered something in Spanish, but the landlord, who reappeared to place Guest's supper on a table on the veranda, here felt the obligation of interfering to protect a customer apparently so aggressive and so opulent. He pushed the inquisitor aside, with a few hasty words, and, after Guest had finished his meal, offered to show him his room. It was a dark vaulted closet on the ground-floor, gaining light from the stable-yard through a barred iron grating. At the first glimpse it looked like a prison cell; looking more deliberately at the black tresseled bed, and the votive images hanging on the wall, it might have been a tomb.

"It is the best," said the landlord. "The Padre Vincento will have none other on his journey."

"I suppose God protects him," said Guest; "that door don't."

He pointed to the worm-eaten door, without bolt or fastening.

"Ah, what matter! Are we not all friends?"

"Certainly," responded Guest, with his surliest manner, as he returned to the veranda. Nevertheless, he resolved not to occupy the cell of the reverend Padre; not from any personal fear of his disreputable neighbors, though he was fully alive to their peculiarities, but from the nomadic instinct which was still strong in his blood. He felt he could not yet bear the confinement of a close room or the propinquity of his fellow-man. He would rest on the veranda until the moon was fairly up, and then he would again take to the road.

He was half reclining on the bench, with the slowly closing and opening lids of some tired but watchful animal, when the sound of wheels, voices, and clatter of hoofs on the highway arrested his attention, and he sat upright. The moon was slowly lifting itself over the limitless stretch of grain-fields before him on the other side of the road, and dazzling him with its level lustre. He could barely discern a cavalcade of dark figures and a large vehicle rapidly approaching, before it drew up tumultuously in front of the fonda.

It was a pleasure party of ladies and gentlemen on horseback and in a four-horsed char-a-bancs returning to La Mision Perdida. Buchanan, Raymond, and Garnier were there; Amita and Dorotea in the body of the char-a-bancs, and Maruja seated on the box. Much to his own astonishment and that of some others of the party, Captain Carroll was among the riders. Only Maruja and her mother knew that he was recalled to refute a repetition of the gossip already circulated regarding his sudden withdrawal; only Maruja alone knew the subtle words which made that call so potent yet so hopeless.

Maruja's quick eyes, observant of everything, even under the double fire of Captain Carroll and Garnier, instantly caught those of the erect figure on the bench in the veranda. Surely that was the face of the tramp she had spoken to! and yet there was a change, not only in the dress but in the general resemblance. After the first glance, Guest withdrew his eyes and gazed at the other figures in the char-a-bancs without moving a muscle.

Maruja's whims and caprices were many and original; and when, after a sudden little cry and a declaration that she could stand her cramped position no longer, she leaped from the box into the road, no one was surprised. Garnier and Captain Carroll quickly followed.

"I should like to look into the fonda while the horses are being watered," she said, laughingly, "just to see what it is that attracts Pereo there so often." Before any one could restrain this new caprice, she was already upon the veranda.

To reach the open door, she had to pass so near Guest that her soft white flounces brushed his knees, and the flowers in her girdle left their perfume in his face. But he neither moved nor raised his eyes. When she had passed, he rose quietly and stepped into the road.

On her nearer survey, Maruja was convinced it was the same man. She remained for an instant, with a little hand on the door-post. "What a horrid place, and what dreadful people!" she said in audible English as she glanced quickly after Guest. "Really, Pereo ought to be warned against keeping such company. Come, let us go."

She contrived to pass Guest again in regaining the carriage; but in the few moments' further delay he walked on down the road before them, and, by the time they were ready to start, he was slowly sauntering some hundred yards ahead. They passed him at a rapid trot, but the next moment the char-a-bancs was suddenly pulled up.

"My fan!" cried Maruja. "Blessed Santa Maria!—my fan!"

A small black object, seen distinctly in the moonlight, was lying on the road, directly in the track of the sauntering stranger. Garnier attempted to alight; Carroll reined in his horse.

"Stop, all of you!" said Maruja; "that man will bring it to me."

It seemed as if he would. He stopped and picked it up, and approached the carriage. Maruja stood up in her seat, with her veil thrown back, her graceful hand extended, her eyes and mouth tremulous with an irresistible smile. The stranger came nearer, singled out Captain Carroll, tossed the fan to him with a slight nod, and passed on the other side.

"One moment," said Maruja, almost harshly, to the driver. "One moment," she continued, drawing her purse from her pocket brusquely. "Let me reward this civil gentleman of the road! Here, sir;" but, before she could continue, Carroll wheeled to her side, and interposed. "Pray collect yourself, Miss Saltonstall," he said, hurriedly; "you can not tell who this man may be. He does not seem to be one who would insult you, or whom YOU would insult gratuitously."

"Give me the fan, Captain Carroll," she said, with a soft and caressing smile. "Thank you." She took it, and, breaking it through the middle between her gloved hands, tossed it into the highway. "You are right—it smells of the fonda—and the road. Thank you, again. You are so thoughtful for me, Captain Carroll," she murmured, raising her eyes gently to his, and then suddenly withdrawing them with a half sigh. "But I am keeping you all. Go on."

The carriage rolled away and Guest returned from the hedge to the middle of the road. San Jose lay in the opposite direction from the disappearing cavalcade; but, on leaving the fonda, he had determined to lead his inquisitors astray by doubling and making a circuit of the hostelry through the fields hidden in the tall grain. This he did, securely passing them within sound of their voices, and was soon well on his way again. He avoided the highway, and, striking a trail through the meadows, diverged to the right, where the low towers and brown walls of a ruined mission church rose above the plain. This would enable him to escape any direct pursuit on the high road, besides, from its slight elevation, giving him a more extended view of the plain. As he neared it, he was surprised to see that, although it was partly dismantled, and the roof had fallen in the central aisle, a part of it was still used as a chapel, and a light was burning behind a narrow opening, partly window and partly shrine. He was almost upon it, when the figure of a man who had been kneeling beneath, with his back towards him, rose, crossed himself devoutly, and stood upright. Before he could turn, Guest disappeared round the angle of the wall, and the tall erect figure of the solitary worshiper passed on without heeding him.

But if Guest had been successful in evading the observation of the man he had come so suddenly upon, he was utterly unconscious of another figure that had been tracking HIM for the last ten minutes through the tall grain, and had even succeeded in gaining the shadow of the wall behind him; and it was this figure, and not his own, that eventually attracted the attention of the tall stranger. The pursuing figure was rapidly approaching the unconscious Guest; in another moment it would have been upon him, when it was suddenly seized from behind by the tall devotee. There was a momentary struggle, and then it freed itself, with the exclamation, "Pereo!"

"Yes—Pereo!" said the old man, panting from his exertions. "And thou art Miguel. So thou wouldst murder a man for a few pesos!" he said, pointing to the knife which the desperado had hurriedly hid in his jacket, "and callest thyself a Californian!"

"'Tis only an Americano—a runaway, with some ill-gotten gold," said Miguel, sullenly, yet with unmistakable fear of the old man. "Besides, it was only to frighten him, the braggart. But since thou fearest to touch a hair of those interlopers—"

"Fearest!" said Pereo, fiercely, clutching him by the throat, and forcing him against the wall. "Fearest! sayest thou. I, Pereo, fear? Dost thou think I would soil these hands, that might strike a higher quarry, with blood of thy game?"

"Forgive me, padrono," gasped Miguel, now thoroughly alarmed at the old man's awakened passion; "pardon; I meant that, since thou knowest him—"

"I know him?" repeated Pereo scornfully, contemptuously throwing Miguel aside, who at once took that opportunity to increase his distance from the old man's arm. "I know him? Thou shalt see. Come hither, child," he called, beckoning to Guest. "Come hither, thou hast nothing to fear now."

Guest, who had been attracted by the sound of altercation behind him, but who was utterly unconscious of its origin or his own relation to it, came forward impatiently. As he did so, Miguel took to his heels. The act did not tend to mollify Guest's surly suspicions, and, pausing a few feet from the old

Bret Harte

man, he roughly demanded his business with him.

Pereo raised his head, with the dignity of years and habits of command. The face of the young man confronting him was clearly illuminated by the moonlight. Pereo's eyes suddenly dilated, his mouth stiffened, he staggered back against the wall.

"Who are you?" he gasped, in uncertain English.

Believing himself the subject of some drunkard's pastime, Guest replied, savagely, "One who has enough of this d—d nonsense, and will stand no more of it from any one, young or old," and turned abruptly on his heel.

"Stay, one moment, Senor, for the love of God!"

Some keen accent of agony in the old man's voice touched even Guest's selfish nature. He halted.

"You are—a stranger here?"—faltered Pereo. "Yes?"

"I am."

"You do not live here?—you have no friends?"

"I told you I am a stranger. I never was here before in my life," said Guest, impatiently.

"True; I am a fool," said the old man, hurriedly, to himself. "I am mad—mad! It is not HIS voice. No! It is not HIS look, now that his face changes. I am crazy." He stopped, and passed his trembling hands across his eyes. "Pardon, Senor," he continued, recalling himself with a humility that was almost ironical in its extravagance. "Pardon, pardon! Yet, perhaps it is not too much to have wanted to know who was the man one has saved."

"Saved!" repeated Guest, with incredulous contempt.

"Ay!" said Pereo, haughtily, drawing his figure erect; ay, saved! Senor." He stopped and shrugged his shoulders. "But let it pass—I say—let it pass. Take an old man's advice, friend: show not your gold hereafter to strangers lightly, no matter how lightly you have come by it. Good-night!"

Guest for a moment hesitated whether to resent the old man's speech, or to let it pass as the incoherent fancy of a brain maddened by drink. Then he ended the discussion by turning his back abruptly and continuing his way to the high-road.

"So!" said Pereo, looking after him with abstracted eyes, "so! it was only a fancy. And yet—even now, as he turned away, I saw the same cold insolence in his eye. Caramba! Am I mad—mad—that I must keep forever before my eyes, night and day, the image of that dog in every outcast, every ruffian, every wayside bully that I meet? No, no, good Pereo! Softly! this is mere madness, good Pereo," he murmured to himself; "thou wilt have none of it; none, good Pereo. Come, come!" He let his head fall slowly forward on his breast, and in that action, seeming to take up again the burden of a score more years upon his shoulders, he moved slowly away.

When he entered the fonda half an hour later, the awe in which he was held by the half superstitious ruffians appeared to have increased. Whatever story the fugitive Miguel had told his companions regarding Pereo's protection of the young stranger, it was certain that it had its full effect. Obsequious to the last degree, the landlord was so profoundly touched, when Pereo, not displeased with this evidence of his power over his countrymen, condescendingly offered to click glasses with him, that he endeavored to placate him still further.

"It is a pity your worship was not here earlier," he began, with a significant glance at the others, "to have seen a gallant young stranger that was here. A spice of wickedness about him, truly—a kind of Don Caesar—but bearing himself like a very caballero always. It would have pleased your worship, who likes not those canting Puritans such as our neighbor yonder."

"Ah," said Pereo, reflectively, warming under the potent fires of flattery and aguardiente, "possibly I HAVE seen him. He was like—"

"Like none of the dogs thou hast seen about San Antonio," interrupted the landlord. "Scarcely did he seem Americano, though he spoke no Spanish."

The old man chuckled to himself viciously. "And thou, thou old fool, Pereo, must needs see a likeness to thine enemy in this poor runaway child—this fugitive Don Juan! He! he!" Nevertheless, he still felt a vague terror of the condition of mind which had produced this fancy, and drank so deeply to dispel his nervousness that it was with difficulty he could mount his horse again. The exaltation of liquor, however, appeared only to intensify his characteristics: his face became more lugubrious and melancholy; his manner more ceremonious and dignified; and, erect and stiff in his saddle from the waist upwards, but leaning from side to side with the motion of his horse, like the tall mast of some laboring sloop, he "loped" away towards the House of the Lost Mission. Once or twice he broke into sentimental song. Strangely enough, his ditty was a popular Spanish refrain of some matador's aristocratic inamorata:—

Do you see my black eyes?
I am Manuel's Duchess,—

sang Pereo, with infinite gravity. His horse's hoofs seemed to keep time with the refrain, and he occasionally waved in the air the long leather thong of his bridle-rein.

It was quite late when he reached La Mision Perdida. Turning into the little lane that led to the stable-yard, he dismounted at a gate in the hedge which led to the summerhouse of the old Mision garden, and, throwing his reins on his mustang's neck, let the animal precede him to the stables. The moon shone full on the inclosure as he emerged from the labyrinth. With uncovered head he approached the Indian mound, and sank on his knees before it.

The next moment he rose, with an exclamation of terror, and his hat dropped from his trembling hand. Directly before him, a small, gray, wolfish-looking animal had stopped half-way down the mound on encountering his motionless figure. Frightened by his outcry, and unable to retreat, the shadowy depredator had fallen back on his slinking haunches with a snarl, and bared teeth that glittered in the moonlight.

In an instant the expression of terror on the old man's ashen face turned into a fixed look of insane exaltation. His white lips moved; he advanced a step further, and held out both hands towards the crouching animal.

"So! It is thou—at last! And comest thou here thy tardy Pereo to chide? Comest THOU, too, to tell the poor old man his heart is cold, his limbs are feeble, his brain weak and dizzy? that he is no longer fit to do thy master's work? Ay, gnash thy teeth at him! Curse him!—curse him in thy throat! But listen!—listen, good friend—I will tell thee a secret—ay, good gray friar, a secret—such a secret! A plan, all mine—

fresh from this old gray head; ha! ha!—all mine! To be wrought by these poor old arms; ha! ha! All mine! Listen!"

He stealthily made a step nearer the affrighted animal. With a sudden sidelong snap, it swiftly bounded by his side, and vanished in the thicket; and Pereo, turning wildly, with a moan sank down helplessly on the grave of his forefathers.

CHAPTER VI

To the open chagrin of most of the gentlemen and the unexpected relief of some of her own sex, Maruja, after an evening of more than usual caprice and willfulness, retired early to her chamber. Here she beguiled Enriquita, a younger sister, to share her solitude for an hour, and with a new and charming melancholy presented her with mature counsel and some younger trinkets and adornments.

"Thou wilt find them but folly, 'Riquita; but thou art young, and wilt outgrow them as I have. I am sick of the Indian beads, everybody wears them; but they seem to suit thy complexion. Thou art not yet quite old enough for jewelry; but take thy choice of these." "'Ruja," replied Enriquita, eagerly, "surely thou wilt not give up this necklace of carved amber, that was brought thee from Manilla—it becomes thee so! Everybody says it. All the caballeros, Raymond and Victor, swear that it sets off thy beauty like nothing else." "When thou knowest men better," responded Maruja, in a deep voice, "thou wilt care less for what they say, and despise what they do. Besides, I wore it to-day—and—I hate it." "But what fan wilt thou keep thyself? The one of sandal-wood thou hadst to-day?" continued Enriquita, timidly eying the pretty things upon the table. "None," responded Maruja, didactically, "but the simplest, which I shall buy myself. Truly, it is time to set one's self against this extravagance.

Girls think nothing of spending as much upon a fan as would buy a horse and saddle for a poor man." "But why so serious tonight, my sister?" said the little Enriquita, her eyes filling with ready tears. "It grieves me," responded Maruja, promptly, "to find thee, like the rest, giving thy soul up to the mere glitter of the world. However, go, child, take the heads, but leave the amber; it would make thee yellower than thou art; which the blessed Virgin forbid! Good-night!"

She kissed her affectionately, and pushed her from the room. Nevertheless, after a moment's survey of her lonely chamber, she hastily slipped on a pale satin dressing-gown, and, darting across the passage, dashed into the bedroom of the youngest Miss Wilson, haled that sentimental brunette from her night toilet, dragged her into her own chamber, and, enwrapping her in a huge mantle of silk and gray fur, fed her with chocolates and chestnuts, and, reclining on her sympathetic shoulder, continued her arraignment of the world and its follies until nearly daybreak.

It was past noon when Maruja awoke, to find Faquita standing by her bedside with ill-concealed impatience.

"I ventured to awaken the Dona Maruja," she said, with vivacious alacrity, "for news! Terrible news! The American, Dr. West, is found dead this morning in the San Jose road!"

"Dr. West dead!" repeated Maruja, thoughtfully, but without emotion.

"Surely dead—very dead. He was thrown from his horse and dragged by the stirrups—how far, the Blessed Virgin only knows. But he is found dead—this Dr. West—his foot in the broken stirrup, his hand holding a piece of the bridle! I thought I would waken the Dona Maruja, that no one else should break it to the Dona Maria."

"That no one else should break it to my mother?" repeated Maruja, coldly. "What mean you, girl?"

"I mean that no stranger should tell her," stammered Faquita, lowering her bold eyes.

"You mean," said Maruja, slowly, "that no silly, staring, tongue-wagging gossip should dare to break upon the morning devotions of the lady mother with open-mouthed tales of horror! You are wise, Faquita! I will tell her myself. Help me to dress."

But the news had already touched the outer shell of the great house, and little groups of the visitors were discussing it upon the veranda. For once, the idle badinage of a pleasure-seeking existence was suspended; stupid people with facts came to the fore; practical people with inquiring minds became interesting; servants were confidentially appealed to; the local expressman became a hero, and it was even noticed that he was intelligent and good-looking.

"What makes it more distressing," said Raymond, joining one of the groups, "is, that it appears the Doctor visited Mrs. Saltonstall last evening, and left the casa at eleven. Sanchez, who was perhaps the last person who saw him alive, says that he noticed his horse was very violent, and the Doctor did not seem able to control him. The accident probably happened half an hour later, as he was picked up about three miles from here, and from appearances must have been dragged, with his foot in the stirrup, fully half a mile before the girth broke and freed the saddle and stirrup together. The mustang, with nothing on but his broken bridle, was found grazing at the rancho as early as four o'clock, an hour before the body of his master was discovered by the men sent from the rancho to look for him."

"Eh, but the man must have been clean daft to have trusted himself to one of those savage beasts of the country," said Mr. Buchanan. "And he was no so young either—about sixty, I should say. It didna look even respectable, I remember, when we met him the other day, careering over the country for all the world like one of those crazy Mexicans. And yet he seemed steady and sensible enough when he didna let his schemes of 'improvements' run away with him like yon furious beastie. Eh well, puir man—it was a sudden ending! And his family—eh?"

"I don't think he has one—at least here," said Raymond. "You can't always tell in California. I believe he was a widower."

"Ay, man, but the heirs; there must be considerable property?" said Buchanan, impatiently.

"Oh, the heirs. If he's made no will, which doesn't look like so prudent and practical a man as he was—the heirs will probably crop up some day."

"PROBABLY! crop up some day," repeated Buchanan, aghast.

"Yes. You must remember that WE don't take heirs quite as much into account as you do in the old country. The loss of the MAN, and how to replace HIM, is much more to us than the disposal of his property. Now, Doctor West was a power far beyond his actual possessions—and we will know very soon how much those were dependent upon him."

"What do you mean?" asked Buchanan, anxiously.

"I mean that five minutes after the news of the Doctor's death was confirmed, your friend Mr. Stanton sent a messenger with a despatch to the nearest telegraphic office, and that he himself drove over to catch Aladdin before the news could reach him."

Buchanan looked uneasy; so did one or two of the native Californians who composed the group, and who had been listening attentively. "And where is this same telegraphic office?" asked Buchanan, cautiously.

"I'll drive you over there presently," responded Raymond, grimly. "There'll be nothing doing here to-day. As Dr. West was a near neighbor of the family, his death suspends our pleasure-seeking until after the funeral."

Mr. Buchanan moved away. Captain Carroll and Garnier drew nearer the speaker. "I trust it will not withdraw from us the society of Miss Saltonstall," said Garnier, lightly—"at least, that she will not be inconsolable."

"She did not seem to be particularly sympathetic with Dr. West the other day," said Captain Carroll, coloring slightly with the recollection of the morning in the summer-house, yet willing, in his hopeless passion, even to share that recollection with his rival. "Did you not think so, Monsieur Garnier?"

"Very possibly; and, as Miss Saltonstall is quite artless and childlike in the expression of her likes and dislikes," said Raymond, with the faintest touch of irony, "you can judge as well as I can."

Garnier parried the thrust lightly. "You are no kinder to our follies than you are to the grand passions of these gentlemen. Confess, you frightened them horribly. You are—what is called—a bear—eh? You depreciate in the interests of business."

Raymond did not at first appear to notice the sarcasm. "I only stated," he said, gravely, "that which these gentlemen will find out for themselves before they are many hours older. Dr. West was the brain of the county, as Aladdin is its life-blood. It only remains to be seen how far the loss of that brain affects the county. The Stock Exchange market in San Francisco will indicate that today in the shares of the San Antonio and Soquel Railroad and the West Mills and Manufacturing Co. It is a matter that may affect even our friends here. Whatever West's social standing was in this house, lately he was in confidential business relations with Mrs. Saltonstall." He raised his eyes for the first time to Garnier as he added, slowly, "It is to be hoped that if our hostess has no social reasons to deplore the loss of Dr. West, she at least will have no other."

With a lover's instinct, conscious only of some annoyance to Maruja, in all this, Carroll anxiously looked for her appearance among the others. He was doomed to disappointment, however. His half-timid inquiries only resulted in the information that Maruja was closeted with her mother. The penetralia of the casa was only accessible to the family; yet, as he wandered uneasily about, he could not help passing once or twice before the quaint low archway, with its grated door, that opened from the central hall. His surprise may be imagined when he suddenly heard his name uttered in a low voice; and, looking up, he beheld the soft eyes of Maruja at the grating.

She held the door partly open with one little hand, and made a sign for him to enter with the other. When he had done so, she said, "Come with me," and preceded him down the dim corridor. His heart beat thickly; the incense of this sacred inner life, with its faint suggestion of dead rose-leaves, filled him with a voluptuous languor; his breath was lost, as if a soft kiss had taken it away; his senses swam in the light mist that seemed to suffuse everything. His step trembled as she suddenly turned aside, and, opening a door, ushered him into a small vaulted chamber.

In the first glance it seemed to be an oratory or chapel. A large gold and ebony crucifix hung on the wall. There was a prie-dieu of heavy dark mahogany in the centre of the tiled floor; there was a low ottoman or couch, covered with a mantle of dark violet velvet, like a pall; there were two quaintly carved stiff chairs; a religious, almost ascetic, air pervaded the apartment; but no dreamy eastern seraglio could have affected him with an intoxication so profoundly and mysteriously sensuous.

Maruja pointed to a chair, and then, with a peculiarly feminine movement, placed herself sideways upon the ottoman, half reclining on her elbow on a high cushion, her deep billowy flounces partly veiling the funereal velvet below. Her oval face was pale and melancholy, her eyes moist as if with recent tears; an expression as of troubled passion lurked in their depths and in the corners of her mouth. Scarcely knowing why, Carroll fancied that thus she might appear if she were in love; and the daring thought made him tremble.

"I wanted to speak with you alone," she said, gently, as if in explanation; "but don't look at me so. I have had a bad night, and now this calamity"—she stopped and then added, softly, "I want you to do a favor for—my mother?"

Captain Carroll, with an effort, at last found his voice. "But YOU are in trouble; YOU are suffering. I had no idea this unfortunate affair came so near to you."

"Nor did I," said Maruja, closing her fan with a slight snap. "I knew nothing of it until my mother told me this morning.

To be frank with you, it now appears that Dr. West was her most intimate business adviser. All her affairs were in his hands. I cannot expain how, or why, or when; but it is so."

"And is that all?" said Carroll, with boyish openness of relief. "And you have no other sorrow?"

In spite of herself, a tender smile, such as she might have bestowed on an impulsive boy, broke on her lips. "And is that not enough? What would you? No—sit where you are! We are here to talk seriously. And you do not ask what is this favor my mother wishes?"

"No matter what it is, it shall be done," said Carroll, quickly. "I am your mother's slave if she will but let me serve at your side. Only," he paused, "I wish it was not business—I know nothing of business."

"If it were only business, Captain Carroll," said Maruja, slowly, "I would have spoken to Raymond or the Senor Buchanan; if it were only confidence, Pereo, our mayor-domo, would have dragged himself from his sick-bed this morning to do my mother's bidding. But it is more than that—it is the functions of a gentleman—and my mother, Captain Carroll, would like to say of—a friend."

He seized her hand and covered it with kisses. She withdrew it gently.

"What have I to do?" he asked, eagerly.

She drew a note from her belt. "It is very simple. You must ride over to Aladdin with that note. You must give it to him ALONE—more than that, you must not let any one who may be there think you are making any but a social call. If he keeps you to dine—you must stay—you will bring back anything he may give you and deliver it to me secretly for her."

"Is that all?" asked Carroll, with a slight touch of disappointment in his tone.

"No," said Maruja, rising impulsively. "No, Captain Carroll—it is NOT all! And you shall know all, if only to prove to you how we confide in you—and to leave you free, after you have heard it, to do as you please." She stood before him, quite white, opening and shutting her fan quickly, and tapping the tiled floor with her little foot. "I have told you Dr. West was my mother's business adviser. She looked upon him as more—as a friend. Do you know what a dangerous thing it is for a woman who has lost one protector to begin to rely upon another? Well, my mother is not yet old. Dr. West appreciated her—Dr. West did not depreciate himself—two things that go far with a woman, Captain Carroll, and my mother is a woman." She paused, and then, with a light toss of her fan, said: "Well, to make an end, but for this excellent horse and this too ambitious rider, one knows not how far the old story of my mother's first choice would have been repeated, and the curse of Koorotora again fallen on the land."

"And you tell me this—you, Maruja—you who warned me against my hopeless passion for you?"

"Could I foresee this?" she said, passionately; "and are you mad enough not to see that this very act would have made YOUR suit intolerable to my relations?"

"Then you did think of my suit, Maruja," he said, grasping her hand.

"Or any one's suit," she continued, hurriedly, turning away

with a slight increase of color in her cheeks. After a moment's pause, she added, in a gentler and half-reproachful voice, "Do you think I have confided my mother's story to you for this purpose only? Is this the help you proffer?"

"Forgive me, Maruja," said the young officer, earnestly. "I am selfish, I know—for I love you. But you have not told me yet how I could help your mother by delivering this letter, which any one could do."

"Let me finish then," said Maruja. "It is for you to judge what may be done. Letters have passed between my mother and Dr. West. My mother is imprudent; I know not what she may have written, or what she might not write, in confidence. But you understand, they are not letters to be made public nor to pass into any hands but hers. They are not to be left to be bandied about by his American friends; to be commented upon by strangers; to reach the ears of the Guitierrez. They belong to that grave which lies between the Past and my mother; they must not rise from it to haunt her."

"I understand," said the young officer, quietly. "This letter, then, is my authority to recover them?"

"Partly, though it refers to other matters. This Mr. Prince, whom you Americans call Aladdin, was a friend of Dr. West; they were associated in business, and he will probably have access to his papers. The rest we must leave to you."

"I think you may," said Carroll, simply.

Maruja stretched out her hand. The young man bent over it respectfully and moved towards the door.

She had expected him to make some protestation—perhaps even to claim some reward. But the instinct which made him forbear even in thought to take advantage of the duty laid upon him, which dominated even his miserable passion for her, and made it subservient to his exaltation of honor; this epaulet of the officer, and blood of the gentleman, this simple possession of knighthood not laid on by perfunctory steel, but springing from within—all this, I grieve to say, was partly unintelligible to Maruja, and not entirely satisfactory. Since he had entered the room they seemed to have changed their situations; he was no longer the pleading lover that trembled at her feet. For one base moment she thought it was the result of his knowledge of her mother's weakness; but the next instant, meeting his clear glance, she colored with shame. Yet she detained him vaguely a moment before the grated door in the secure shadow of the arch. He might have kissed her there! He did not.

In the gloomy stagnation of the great house, it was natural that he should escape from it for a while, and the saddling of his horse for a solitary ride attracted no attention. But it might have been noticed that his manner had lost much of that nervous susceptibility and anxiety which indicates a lover; and it was with a return of his professional coolness and precision that he rode out of the patio as if on parade. Erect, observant, and self-possessed, he felt himself "on duty," and, putting spurs to his horse, cantered along the high-road, finding an inexpressible relief in motion. He was doing something in the interest of helplessness and of HER. He had no doubt of his right to interfere. He did not bother himself with the rights of others. Like all self-contained men, he had no plan of action, except what the occasion might suggest.

He was more than two miles from La Mision Perdida, when his quick eye was attracted by a saddle-blanket lying in the roadside ditch. A recollection of the calamity of the previous night made him rein in his horse and examine it. It was

Bret Harte

without doubt the saddle-blanket of Dr. West's horse, lost when the saddle came off, after the Doctor's body had been dragged by the runaway beast. But a second fact forced itself equally upon the young officer. It was lying nearly a mile from the spot where the body had been picked up. This certainly did not agree with the accepted theory that the accident had taken place further on, and that the body had been dragged until the saddle came off where it was found. His professional knowledge of equitation and the technique of accoutrements exploded the idea that the saddle could have slipped here, the saddle-blanket fallen and the horse have run nearly a mile hampered by the saddle hanging under him. Consequently, the saddle, blanket, and unfortunate rider must have been precipitated together, and at the same moment, on or near this very spot. Captain Carroll was not a detective; he had no theory to establish, no motive to discover, only as an officer, he would have simply rejected any excuse offered on those terms by one of his troopers to account for a similar accident. He troubled himself with no further deduction. Without dismounting, he gave a closer attention to the marks of struggling hoofs near the edge of the ditch, which had not yet been obliterated by the daily travel. In doing so, his horse's hoof struck a small object partly hidden in the thick dust of the highway. It seemed to be a leather letter or memorandum case adapted for the breast pocket. Carroll instantly dismounted and picked it up. The name and address of Dr. West were legibly written on the inside. It contained a few papers and notes, but nothing more. The possibility that it might disclose the letters he was seeking was a hope quickly past. It was only a corroborative fact that the accident had taken place on the spot where he was standing. He was losing time; he hurriedly put the book in his pocket, and once more spurred forward on his road.

CHAPTER VII

The exterior of Aladdin's Palace, familiar as it already was to Carroll, struck him that afternoon as looking more than usually unreal, ephemeral, and unsubstantial. The Moorish arches, of the thinnest white pine; the arabesque screens and lattices that looked as if made of pierced cardboard; the golden minarets that seemed to be glued to the shell-like towers, and the hollow battlements that visibly warped and cracked in the fierce sunlight,—all appeared more than ever like a theatrical scene that might sink through the ground, or vanish on either side to the sound of the prompter's whistle. Recalling Raymond's cynical insinuations, he could not help fancying that the house had been built by a conscientious genie with a view to the possibility of the lamp and the ring passing, with other effects, into the hands of the sheriff.

Nevertheless, the servant who took Captain Carroll's horse summoned another domestic, who preceded him into a small waiting-room off the gorgeous central hall, which looked not unlike the private bar-room of a first-class hotel, and presented him with a sherry cobbler. It was a peculiarity of Aladdin's Palace that the host seldom did the honors of his own house, but usually deputed the task to some friend, and generally the last new-comer. Carroll was consequently not surprised when he was presently joined by an utter stranger, who again pressed upon him the refreshment he had just

Bret Harte

declined. "You see," said the transitory host, "I'm a stranger myself here, and haven't got the ways of the regular customers; but call for anything you like, and I'll see it got for you. Jim" (the actual Christian name of Aladdin) "is headin' a party through the stables. Would you like to join 'em—they ain't more than half through now—or will you come right to the billiard-room—the latest thing out in stained glass and iron—ez pretty as fresh paint? or will you meander along to the bridal suite, and see the bamboo and silver dressing-room, and the white satin and crystal bed that cost fifteen thousand dollars as it stands. Or," he added, confidentially, "would you like to cut the whole cussed thing, and I'll get out Jim's 2.32 trotter and his spider-legged buggy and we'll take a spin over to the Springs afore dinner?" It was, however, more convenient to Carroll's purpose to conceal his familiarity with the Aladdin treasures, and to politely offer to follow his guide through the house. "I reckon Jim's pretty busy just now," continued the stranger; "what with old Doc West going under so suddent, just ez he'd got things boomin' with that railroad and his manufactory company. The stocks went down to nothing this morning; and, 'twixt you and me, the boys say," he added, mysteriously sinking his voice, "it was jest the tightest squeeze there whether there wouldn't be a general burst-up all round. But Jim was over at San Antonio afore the Doctor's body was laid out; just ran that telegraph himself for about two hours; had a meeting of trustees and directors afore the Coroner came; had the Doctor's books and papers brought over here in a buggy, and another meeting before luncheon. Why, by the time the other fellows began to drop in to know if the Doctor was really dead, Jim Prince had discounted the whole affair two years ahead. Why, bless you, nearly everybody is in it. That Spanish woman over there, with the pretty daughter—that high-toned Greaser with the big house—you know who I mean." . . .

"I don't think I do," said Carroll, coldly. "I know a lady named Saltonstall, with several daughters."

"That's her; thought I'd seen you there once. Well, the Doctor's got her into it, up to the eyes. I reckon she's mortgaged everything to him."

It required all Carroll's trained self-possession to prevent his garrulous guide from reading his emotion in his face. This, then, was the secret of Maruja's melancholy. Poor child! how bravely she had borne up under it; and HE, in his utter selfishness, had never suspected it. Perhaps that letter was her delicate way of breaking the news to him, for he should certainly now hear it all from Aladdin's lips. And this man, who evidently had succeeded to the control of Dr. West's property, doubtless had possession of the letters too! Humph! He shut his lips firmly together, and strode along by the side of his innocent guide, erect and defiant.

He did not have long to wait. The sound of voices, the opening of doors, and the trampling of feet indicated that the other party were being "shown over" that part of the building Carroll and his companion were approaching. "There's Jim and his gang now," said his cicerone; "I'll tell him you're here, and step out of this show business myself. So long! I reckon I'll see you at dinner." At this moment Prince and a number of ladies and gentlemen appeared at the further end of the hall; his late guide joined them, and apparently indicated Carroll's presence, as, with a certain lounging, off-duty, officer-like way, the young man sauntered on.

Aladdin, like others of his class, objected to the military, theoretically and practically; but he was not above recognizing their social importance in a country of no society, and of even being fascinated by Carroll's quiet and secure self-possession and self-contentment in a community of restless ambition and aggressive assertion. He came forward to welcome him cordially; he introduced him with an air of satisfaction; he would have preferred if he had been in uniform, but he contented himself with the fact that Carroll, like all men of disciplined limbs, carried himself equally well in mufti.

"You have shown us everything," said Carroll, smiling, "except the secret chamber where you keep the magic lamp and ring. Are we not to see the spot where the incantation that produces these marvels is held, even if we are forbidden to witness the ceremony? The ladies are dying to see your sanctum—your study—your workshop—where you really live."

"You'll find it a mere den, as plain as my bed-room," said Prince, who prided himself on the Spartan simplicity of his own habits, and was not averse to the exhibition. "Come this way." He crossed the hall, and entered a small, plainly furnished room, containing a table piled with papers, some of which were dusty and worn-looking. Carroll instantly conceived the idea that these were Dr. West's property. He took his letter quietly from his pocket; and, when the attention of the others was diverted, laid it on the table, with the remark, in an undertone, audible only to Prince, "From Mrs. Saltonstall."

Aladdin had that sublime audacity which so often fills the place of tact. Casting a rapid glance at Carroll, he cried, "Hallo!" and, wheeling suddenly round on his following guests, with a bewildering extravagance of playful brusque-ness, actually bundled them from the room. "The incantation is on!" he cried, waving his arms in the air; "the genie is at work. No admittance except on business! Follow Miss Wilson," he added, clapping both hands on the shoulders of the prettiest and shyest young lady of the party, with an irresistible paternal familiarity. "She's your hostess. I'll honor her drafts to any amount;" and before they were aware of his purpose or that Carroll was no longer among them, Aladdin had closed the door, that shut with a spring lock, and was alone with the young man. He walked quickly to his desk, took up the letter, and opened it.

His face of dominant, self-satisfied good-humor became set and stern. Without taking the least notice of Carroll, he rose, and, stepping to a telegraph instrument at a side table, manipulated half a dozen ivory knobs with a sudden energy. Then he returned to the table, and began hurriedly to glance over the memoranda and indorsements of the files of papers piled upon it. Carroll's quick eye caught sight of a small packet of letters in a writing of unmistakable feminine delicacy, and made certain they were the ones he was in quest of. Without raising his eyes, Mr. Prince asked, almost rudely,—

"Who else has she told this to?"

"If you refer to the contents of that letter, it was written and handed to me about three hours ago. It has not been out of my possession since then."

"Humph! Who's at the casa? There's Buchanan, and Raymond, and Victor Guitierrez, eh?"

"I think I can say almost positively that Mrs. Saltonstall has seen no one but her daughter since the news reached her, if that is what you wish to know," said Carroll, still following the particular package of letters with his eyes, as Mr. Prince continued his examination. Prince stopped.

"Are you sure?"

"Almost sure."

Prince rose, this time with a greater ease of manner, and, going to the table, ran his fingers over the knobs, as if mechanically. "One would like to know at once all there is to know about a transaction that changes the front of four millions of capital in about four hours, eh, Captain?" he said, for the first time really regarding his guest. "Just four hours ago, in this very room, we found out that the widow Saltonstall owed Dr. West about a million, tied up in investments, and we calculated to pull her through with perhaps the loss of half. If she's got this assignment of the Doctor's property that she speaks of in her letter, as collateral security, and it's all regular, and she—so to speak—steps into Dr. West's place, by G-d, sir, we owe HIM about three millions, and we've got to settle with HER—and that's all about it. You've dropped a little bomb-shell in here, Captain, and the splinters are flying around as far as San Francisco, now. I confess it beats me regularly. I always thought the old man was a little keen over there at the casa—but she was a woman, and he was a man for all his sixty years, and THAT combination I never thought of. I only wonder she hadn't gobbled him up before."

Captain Carroll's face betrayed no trace of the bewilderment and satisfaction at this news of which he had been the unconscious bearer, nor of resentment at the coarseness of its translation.

"There does not seem to be any memorandum of this assignment," continued Prince, turning over the papers.

"Have you looked here?" said Carroll, taking up the packet of letters.

"No—they seem to me some private letters she refers to in

this letter, and that she wants back again."

"Let us see," said Carroll, untying the packet. There were three or four closely written notes in Spanish and English.

"Love-letters, I reckon," said Prince—"that's why the old girl wants 'em back. She don't care to have the wheedling that fetched the Doctor trotted out to the public."

"Let us look more carefully," said Carroll, pleasantly, opening each letter before Prince, yet so skillfully as to frustrate any attempt of the latter to read them. "There does not seem to be any memorandum here. They are evidently only private letters."

"Quite so," said Prince.

Captain Carroll retied the packet and put it in his pocket. "Then I'll return them to her," he said, quietly.

"Hullo!—here—I say," said Prince, starting to his feet.

"I said I would return them to her," repeated Carroll, calmly.

"But I never gave them to you! I never consented to their withdrawal from the papers."

"I'm sorry you did not," said Carroll, coldly; "it would have been more polite."

"Polite! D—n it, sir! I call this stealing."

"Stealing, Mr. Prince, is a word that might be used by the person who claims these letters to describe the act of any one who would keep them from HER. It really can not apply to you or me."

"Once for all, do you refuse to return them to me?" said Prince, pale with anger.

"Decidedly."

"Very well, sir! We shall see." He stepped to the corner and rang a bell. "I have summoned my manager, and will charge you with the theft in his presence."

"I think not."

"And why, sir?"

"Because the presence of a third party would enable me to throw this glove in your face, which, as a gentleman, I couldn't do without witnesses." Steps were heard along the passage; Prince was no coward in a certain way; neither was he a fool. He knew that Carroll would keep his word; he knew that he should have to fight him; that, whatever the issue of the duel was, the cause of the quarrel would be known, and scarcely redound to his credit. At present there were no witnesses to the offered insult, and none would be wiser. The letters were not worth it. He stepped to the door, opened it, said, "No matter," and closed it again.

He returned with an affectation of carelessness. "You are right. I don't know that I'm called upon to make a scene here which the LAW can do for me as well elsewhere. It will settle pretty quick whether you've got the right to those letters, and whether you've taken the right way to get them sir."

"I have no desire to evade any responsibility in this matter, legal or otherwise," said Carroll, coldly, rising to his feet.

"Look here," said Prince, suddenly, with a return of his

brusque frankness; "you might have ASKED me for those letters, you know."

"And you wouldn't have given them to me," said Carroll.

Prince laughed. "That's so! I say, Captain. Did they teach you this sort of strategy at West Point?"

"They taught me that I could neither receive nor give an insult under a white flag," said Carroll, pleasantly. "And they allowed me to make exchanges under the same rule. I picked up this pocket-book on the spot where the accident occurred to Dr. West. It is evidently his. I leave it with you, who are his executor."

The instinct of reticence before a man with whom he could never be confidential kept him from alluding to his other discovery.

Prince took the pocket-book, and opened it mechanically. After a moment's scrutiny of the memoranda it contained, his face assumed something of the same concentrated attention it wore at the beginning of the interview. Raising his eyes suddenly to Carroll, he said, quickly,—

"You have examined it?"

"Only so far as to see that it contained nothing of importance to the person I represent," returned Carroll, simply.

The capitalist looked at the young officer's clear eyes. Something of embarrassment came into his own as he turned them away.

"Certainly. Only memoranda of the Doctor's business. Quite important to us, you know. But nothing referring to YOUR principal." He laughed. "Thank you for the exchange. I say—take a drink!"

"Thank you—no!" returned Carroll, going to the door.

"Well, good-by."

He held out his hand. Carroll, with his clear eyes still regarding him, passed quietly by the outstretched hand, opened the door, bowed, and made his exit.

A slight flush came into Prince's cheek. Then, as the door closed, he burst into a half-laugh. Had he been a dramatic villain, he would have added to it several lines of soliloquy, in which he would have rehearsed the fact that the opportunity for revenge had "come at last"; that the "haughty victor who had just left with his ill-gotten spoil had put into his hands the weapon of his friend's destruction"; that the "hour had come"; and, possibly he might have said, "Ha! ha!" But, being a practical, good-natured, selfish rascal, not much better or worse than his neighbors, he sat himself down at his desk and began to carefully consider how HE could best make use of the memoranda jotted down by Dr. West of the proofs of the existence of his son, and the consequent discovery of a legal heir to his property.

CHAPTER VIII

When Faquita had made sure that her young mistress was so securely closeted with Dona Maria that morning as to be inaccessible to curious eyes and ears, she saw fit to bewail to her fellow-servants this further evidence of the decay of the old feudal and patriarchal mutual family confidences. "Time was, thou rememberest, Pepita, when an affair of this kind was openly discussed at chocolate with everybody present, and before us all. When Joaquin Padilla was shot at Monterey, it was the Dona herself who told us, who read aloud the letters describing it and the bullet-holes in his clothes, and made it quite a gala-day—and he was a first-cousin of Guitierrez. And now, when this American goat of a doctor is kicked to death by a mule, the family must shut themselves up, that never a question is asked or answered." "Ay," responded Pepita; "and as regards that, Sanchez there knows as much as they do, for it was he that almost saw the whole affair."

"How?—sawest it?" inquired Faquita, eagerly.

"Why, was it not he that was bringing home Pereo, who had been lying in one of his trances or visions—blessed St. Antonio preserve us!" said Pepita, hastily crossing herself—"on Kooratora's grave, when the Doctor's mustang charged down upon them like a wild bull, and the Doctor's foot half out of the stirrups, and he not yet fast in his seat. And Pereo laughs a wild laugh and says: 'Watch if the coyote does not drag yet at his mustang's heels;' and Sanchez ran and watched the Doctor out of sight, careering and galloping to his death!—ay, as Pereo prophesied. For it was only half an hour afterward that Sanchez again heard the tramp of his hoofs—as if it were here—and knowing it two miles away—thou understandest, he said to himself: 'It is over.'"

The two women shuddered and crossed themselves.

"And what says Pereo of the fulfillment of his prophecy?" asked Faquita, hugging herself in her shawl with a certain titillating shrug of fascinating horror.

"It is even possible he understands it not. Thou knowest how dazed and dumb he ever is after these visions—that he comes from them as one from the grave, remembering nothing. He has lain like a log all the morning."

"Ay; but this news should awaken him, if aught can. He loved not this sneaking Doctor. Let us seek him; mayhap, Sanchez may be there. Come! The mistress lacks us not just now; the guests are provided for. Come!"

She led the way to the eastern angle of the casa communicating by a low corridor with the corral and stables. This was the old "gate-keep" or quarters of the mayordomo, who, among his functions, was supposed to exercise a supervision over the exits and entrances of the house. A large steward's room or office, beyond it a room of general assembly, half guard-room, half servants' hall, and Pereo's sleeping-room, constituted his domain. A few peons were gathered in the hall near the open door of the apartment where Pereo lay.

Stretched on a low pallet, his face yellow as wax, a light

burning under a crucifix near his head, and a spray of blessed palm, popularly supposed to avert the attempts of evil spirits to gain possession of his suspended faculties, Pereo looked not unlike a corpse. Two muffled and shawled domestics, who sat by his side, might have been mourners, but for their voluble and incessant chattering.

"So thou art here, Faquita," said a stout virago. "It is a wonder thou couldst spare time from prayers for the repose of the American Doctor's soul to look after the health of thy superior, poor Pereo! Is it, then, true that Dona Maria said she would have naught more to do with the drunken brute of her mayordomo?"

The awful fascination of Pereo's upturned face did not prevent Faquita from tossing her head as she replied, pertly, that she was not there to defend her mistress from lazy gossip. "Nay, but WHAT said she?" asked the other attendant.

"She said Pereo was to want for nothing; but at present she could not see him."

A murmur of indignation and sympathy passed through the company. It was followed by a long sigh from the insensible man. "His lips move," said Faquita, still fascinated by curiosity. "Hush! he would speak."

"His lips move, but his soul is still asleep," said Sanchez, oracularly. "Thus they have moved since early morning, when I came to speak with him, and found him lying here in a fit upon the floor. He was half dressed, thou seest, as if he had risen to go forth, and had been struck down so—"

"Hush! I tell thee he speaks," said Faquita.

The sick man was faintly articulating through a few tiny bubbles that broke upon his rigid lips. "He—dared—me! He—said—I was old—too old."

"Who dared thee? Who said thou wast too old?" asked the eager Faquita, bending over him.

"He, Koorotora himself! in the shape of a coyote."

Faquita fell back with a little giggle, half of shame, half of awe.

"It is ever thus," said Sanchez, sententiously; "it is what he said last night, when I picked him up on the mound. He will sleep now—thou shalt see. He will get no further than Koorotora and the coyote—and then he will sleep."

And to the awe of the group, and the increased respect for Sanchez's wisdom, Pereo seemed to fall again into a lethargic slumber. It was late in the evening when he appeared to regain perfect consciousness. "Ah—what is this?" he said, roughly, sitting up in bed, and eying the watchers around him, some of whom had succumbed to sleep, and others were engaged in playing cards. "Caramba! are ye mad? Thou, Sanchez, here; who shouldst be at thy work in the stables! Thou, Pepita, is thy mistress asleep or dead, that thou sittest here? Blessed San Antonio! would ye drive me mad?" He lifted his hand to his head, with a dull movement of pain, and attempted to rise from the bed.

"Softly, good Pereo; lie still," said Sanchez, approaching him. "Thou hast been ill—so ill. These, thy friends, have been waiting only for this moment to be assured that thou art better. For this idleness there is no blame—truly none. The Dona Maria has said that thou shouldst lack no care; and, truly, since the terrible news there has been little to do."

"The terrible news?" repeated Pereo.

Sanchez cast a meaning glance upon the others, as if to indicate this coafirmation of his diagnosis.

"Ay, terrible news! The Doctor West was found this morning dead two miles from the casa."

"Dr. West dead!" repeated Pereo, slowly, as if endeavoring to master the real meaning of the words. Then, seeing the vacuity of his question reflected on the faces of those around him, he added, hurriedly, with a feeble smile, "O—ay— dead! Yes! I remember. And he has been ill—very ill, eh?"

"It was an accident. He was thrown from his horse, and so killed," returned Sanchez, gravely.

"Killed—by his horse! sayest thou?" said Pereo, with a sudden fixed look in his eye.

"Ay, good Pereo. Dost thou not remember when the mustang bolted with him down upon us in the lane, and then thou didst say he would come to evil with the brute? He did— blessed San Antonio!—within half an hour!"

"How—thou sawest it?"

"Nay; for the mustang was running away and I did not follow. Bueno! it happened all the same. The Alcalde, Coroner, who knows all about it, has said so an hour ago! Juan brought the news from the rancho where the inquest was. There will be a funeral the day after to-morrow! and so it is that some of the family will go. Fancy, Pereo, a Guitierrez at the funeral of the Americano Doctor! Nay, I doubt not that the Dona Maria will ask thee to say a prayer over his bier."

"Peace, fool! and speak not of thy lady mistress," thundered the old man, sitting upright. "Begone to the stables. Dost thou hear me? Go!"

"Now, by the Mother of Miracles," said Sanchez, hastening from the room as the gaunt figure of the old man rose, like a sheeted spectre, from the bed, "that was his old self again! Blessed San Antonio! Pereo has recovered."

The next day he was at his usual duties, with perhaps a slight increase of sternness in his manner. The fulfillment of his prophecy related by Sanchez added to the superstitious reputation in which he was held, although Faquita voiced the opinions of a growing skeptical party in the statement that it was easy to prophesy the Doctor's accident, with the spectacle of the horse actually running away before the prophet's eyes. It was even said that Dona Maria's aversion to Pereo since the accident arose from a belief that some assistance might have been rendered by him. But it was pointed out by Sanchez that Pereo had, a few moments before, fallen under one of those singular, epileptic-like strokes to which he was subject, and not only was unfit, but even required the entire care of Sanchez at the time. He did not attend the funeral, nor did Mrs. Saltonstall; but the family was represented by Maruja and Amita, accompanied by one or two dark-faced cousins, Captain Carroll, and Raymond. A number of friends and business associates from the neighboring towns, Aladdin and a party from his house, the farm laborers, and a crowd of working men from his mills in the foot-hills, swelled the assemblage that met in and around the rude agricultural sheds and outhouses which formed the only pastoral habitation of the Rancho of San Antonio. It had been a characteristic injunction of the deceased that he should be buried in the midst of one of his most prolific grain fields, as a grim return to that nature he was impoverishing, with neither mark nor monument to indicate the spot; and that even the temporary mound above him should, at the fitting season of the year, be leveled with the rest of the field by the obliterating plowshares. A grave was accordingly dug about a quarter of a mile from his office amidst a "volunteer" crop so dense that the large space mown around the narrow opening, to admit of the presence of the multitude, seemed like a golden amphitheatre.

A distinguished clergyman from San Francisco officiated.

A man of tact and politic adaptation, he dwelt upon the blameless life of the deceased, on his practical benefit for civilization in the county, and even treated his grim Pantheism in the selection of his grave as a formal recognition of the text, "dust to dust." He paid a not ungrateful compliment to the business associates of the deceased, and, without actually claiming in the usual terms "a continuance of past favors" for their successors, managed to interpolate so strong a recommendation of the late Doctor's commercial projects as to elicit from Aladdin the expressive commendation that his sermon was "as good as five per cent. in the stock."

Maruja, who had been standing near the carriage, languidly silent and abstracted even under the tender attentions of Carroll, suddenly felt the consciousness of another pair of eyes fixed upon her. Looking up, she was surprised to find herself regarded by the man she had twice met, once as a tramp and once as a wayfarer at the fonda, who had quietly joined a group not far from her. At once impressed by the idea that this was the first time that he had really looked at her, she felt a singular shyness creeping over her, until, to her own astonishment and indignation, she was obliged to lower her eyes before his gaze. In vain she tried to lift them, with her old supreme power of fascination. If she had ever blushed, she felt she would have done so now. She knew that her face must betray her consciousness; and at last she—Maruja, the self-poised and all-sufficient goddess—actually turned, in half-hysterical and girlish bashfulness, to Carroll for relief in an affected and exaggerated absorption of his attentions. She scarcely knew that the clergyman had finished speaking, when Raymond approached them softly from behind. "Pray don't believe," he said, appealingly, "that all the human virtues are about to be buried—I should say sown—in that wheatfield. A few will still survive, and creep about above the Doctor's grave. Listen to a story just told me, and disbelieve—if you dare—in human gratitude. Do you see that picturesque young ruffian over there?"

Maruja did not lift her eyes. She felt herself breathlessly hanging on the speaker's next words.

"Why, that's the young man of the fonda, who picked up your fan," said Carroll, "isn't it?"

"Perhaps," said Maruja, indifferently. She would have given worlds to have been able to turn coldly and stare at him at that moment with the others, but she dared not. She contented herself with softly brushing some dust from Captain Carroll's arm with her fan and a feminine suggestion of tender care which thrilled that gentleman.

"Well," continued Raymond, "that Robert Macaire over yonder came here some three or four days ago as a tramp, in want of everything but honest labor. Our lamented friend consented to parley with him, which was something remarkable in the Doctor; still more remarkable, he gave him a suit of clothes, and, it is said, some money, and sent him on his way. Now, more remarkable than all, our friend, on hearing of his benefactor's death, actually tramps back here to attend his funeral. The Doctor being dead, his executors not of a kind to emulate the Doctor's spasmodic generosity, and there being no chance of future favors, the act must be recorded as purely and simply gratitude. By Jove! I don't know but that he is the only one here who can be called a real mourner. I'm here because your sister is here; Carroll comes because YOU do, and you come because your mother can not."

"And who tells you these pretty stories?" asked Maruja, with her face still turned towards Carroll.

"The foreman, Harrison, who, with an extensive practical experience of tramps, was struck with this exception to the general rule."

"Poor man; one ought to do something for him," said Amita, compassionately.

"What!" said Raymond, with affected terror, "and spoil this perfect story? Never! If I should offer him ten dollars, I'd expect him to kick me; if he took it, I'd expect to kick HIM."

"He is not so bad-looking, is he, Maruja?" asked Amita of her sister. But Maruja had already moved a few paces off with Carroll, and seemed to be listening to him only. Raymond smiled at the pretty perplexity of Amita's eyebrows over this pronounced indiscretion.

"Don't mind them," he whispered; "you really cannot expect to duena your elder sister. Tell me, would you actually like me to see if I could assist the virtuous tramp? You have only to speak." But Amita's interest appeared to be so completely appeased with Raymond's simple offer that she only smiled, blushed, and said "No."

Maruja's quick ears had taken in every word of these asides, and for an instant she hated her sister for her aimless declination of Raymond's proposal. But becoming conscious —under her eyelids—that the stranger was moving away with the dispersing crowd, she rejoined Amita with her usual manner. The others had re-entered the carriage, but Maruja took it into her head to proceed on foot to the rude building whence the mourners had issued. The foreman, Harrison, flushed and startled by this apparition of inaccessible beauty at his threshold, came eagerly forward. "I shall not trouble you now, Mr. Har-r-r-rison," she said, with a polite exagge- ration of the consonants; "but some day I shall ride over here, and ask you to show me your wonderful machines."

She smiled, and turned back to seek her carriage. But before she had gone many yards she found that she had completely lost it in the intervening billows of grain. She stopped, with an impatient little Spanish ejaculation. The next moment the stalks of wheat parted before her and a figure emerged. It was the stranger.

She fell back a step in utter helplessness.

He, on his side, retreated again into the wheat, holding it back with extended arms to let her pass. As she moved forward mechanically, without a word he moved backward, making a path for her until she was able to discern the coachman's whip above the bending heads of the grain just beyond her. He stopped here and drew to one side, his arms still extended, to give her free passage. She tried to speak, but could only bow her head, and slipped by him with a strange feeling—suggested by his attitude—that she was evading his embrace. But the next moment his arms were lowered, the grain closed around him, and he was lost to her view. She reached the carriage almost unperceived by the inmates, and pounced upon her sister with a laugh.

"Blessed Virgin!" said Amita, "where did you come from?"

"From there!" said Maruja, with a slight nervous shiver, pointing to the clustering grain.

"We were afraid you were lost."

"So was I," said Maruja, raising her pretty lashes heavenwards, as she drew a shawl tightly round her shoulders.

"Has anything happened. You look strange," said Carroll, drawing closer to her.

Here eyes were sparkling, but she was very pale.

"Nothing, nothing!" she said, hastily, glancing at the grain again.

"If it were not that the haste would have been absolutely indecent, I should say that the late Doctor had made you a ghostly visit," said Raymond, looking at her curiously.

"He would have been polite enough not to have commented on my looks," said Maruja. "Am I really such a fright?"

Carroll thought he had never seen her so beautiful. Her eyelids were quivering over their fires as if they had been brushed by the passing wing of a strong passion.

"What are you thinking of?" said Carroll, as they drove on.

She was thinking that the stranger had looked at her admiringly, and that his eyes were blue. But she looked quietly into her lover's face, and said, sweetly, "Nothing, I fear, that would interest you!"

CHAPTER IX

The news of the assignment of Dr. West's property to Mrs. Saltonstall was followed by the still more astonishing discovery that the Doctor's will further bequeathed to her his entire property, after payment of his debts and liabilities. It was given in recognition of her talents and business integrity during their late association, and as an evidence of the confidence and "undying affection" of the testator. Nevertheless, after the first surprise, the fact was accepted by the community as both natural and proper under that singular instinct of humanity which acquiesces without scruple in the union of two large fortunes, but sharply questions the conjunction of poverty and affluence, and looks only for interested motives where there is disparity of wealth. Had Mrs. Saltonstall been a poor widow instead of a rich one; had she been the Doctor's housekeeper instead of his business friend, the bequest would have been strongly criticised—if not legally tested. But this combination, which placed the entire valley of San Antonio in the control of a single individual, appeared to be perfectly legitimate. More than that, some vague rumor of the Doctor's past and his early entanglements only seemed to make this eminently practical disposition of his property the more respectable, and condoned for any moral irregularities of his youth.

The effect upon the collateral branches of the Guitierrez

family and the servants and retainers was even more impressive. For once, it seemed that the fortunes and traditions of the family were changed; the female Guitierrez, instead of impoverishing the property, had augmented it; the foreigner and intruder had been despoiled; the fate of La Mision Perdida had been changed; the curse of Koorotora had proved a blessing; his prophet and descendant, Pereo, the mayordomo, moved in an atmosphere of superstitious adulation and respect among the domestics and common people. This recognition of his power he received at times with a certain exaltation of grandiloquent pride beyond the conception of any but a Spanish servant, and at times with a certain dull, pained vacancy of perception and an expression of frightened bewilderment which also went far to establish his reputation as an unconscious seer and thaumaturgist. "Thou seest," said Sanchez to the partly skeptical Faquita, "he does not know more than an infant what is his power. That is the proof of it." The Dona Maria alone did not participate in this appreciation of Pereo, and when it was proposed that a feast or celebration of rejoicing should be given under the old pear-tree by the Indian's mound, her indignation was long remembered by those that witnessed it. "It is not enough that we have been made ridiculous in the past," she said to Maruja, "by the interference of this solemn fool, but that the memory of our friend is to be insulted by his generosity being made into a triumph of Pereo's idiotic ancestor. One would have thought those coyotes and Koorotora's bones had been buried with the cruel gossip of your relations"—(it had been the recent habit of Dona Maria to allude to "the family" as being particularly related to Maruja alone)—"over my poor friend. Let him beware that his ancestor's mound is not uprooted with the pear-tree, and his heathenish temple destroyed. If, as the engineer says, a branch of the new railroad can be established for La Mision Perdida, I agree with him that it can better pass at that point with less sacrifice to the domain. It is the one uncultivated part of the park, and lies at the proper angle."

"You surely would not consent to this, my mother?" said Maruja, with a sudden impression of a newly found force in her mother's character.

"Why not, child?" said the relict of Mr. Saltonstall and the mourner of Dr. West, coldly. "I admit it was discreet of thee in old times to have thy sentimental passages there with caballeros who, like the guests of the hidalgo that kept a skeleton at his feast, were reminded of the mutability of their hopes by Koorotora's bones and the legend. But with the explosion of this idea of a primal curse, like Eve's, on the property," added the Dona Maria, with a slight bitterness, "thou mayest have thy citas—elsewhere. Thou canst scarcely keep this Captain Carroll any longer at a distance by rattling those bones of Koorotora in his face. And of a truth, child, since the affair of the letters, and his discreet and honorable conduct since, I see not why thou shouldst. He has thy mother's reputation in his hands."

"He is a gentleman, my mother," said Maruja, quietly.

"And they are scarce, child, and should be rewarded and preserved. That is what I meant, silly one; this Captain is not rich—but then, thou hast enough for both."

"But it was Amita that first brought him here," said Maruja, looking down with an air of embarrassed thoughtfulness, which Dona Maria chose to instantly accept as exaggerated coyness.

"Do not think to deceive me or thyself, child, with this folly. Thou art old enough to know a man's mind, if not thine own. Besides, I do not know that I shall object to her liking for Raymond. He is very clever, and would be a relief to some of thy relatives. He would be invaluable to us in the emergencies that may grow out of these mechanical affairs that I do not understand—such as the mill and the railroad."

"And you propose to take a few husbands as partners in the business?" said Maruja, who had recovered her spirits. "I warn you that Captain Carroll is as stupid as a gentleman could be. I wonder that he has not blundered in other things as badly as he has in preferring me to Amita. He confided to me only last night, that he had picked up a pocket-book belonging to the Doctor and given it to Aladdin, without a witness or receipt, and evidently of his own accord."

"A pocket-book of the Doctor's?" repeated Dona Maria.

"Ay; but it contained nothing of thine," said Maruja. "The poor child had sense enough to think of that. But I am in no hurry to ask your consent and your blessing yet, little mother. I could even bear that Amita should precede me to the altar, if the exigencies of thy 'business' require it. It might also secure Captain Carroll for me. Nay, look not at me in that cheapening, commercial way—with compound interest in thine eyes. I am not so poor an investment, truly, of thy original capital."

"Thou art thy father's child," said her mother, suddenly kissing her; "and that is saying enough, the Blessed Virgin knows. Go now," she continued, gently pushing her from the room, "and send Amita hither." She watched the disappearance of Maruja's slightly rebellious shoulders, and added to herself, "And this is the child that Amita really believes is pining with lovesickness for Carroll, so that she can neither sleep nor eat. This is the girl that Faquita would have me think hath no longer any heart in her dress or in her finery! Soul of Joseph Saltonstall!" ejaculated the widow, lifting her shoulders and her eyes together, "thou hast much to account for."

Two weeks later she again astonished her daughter. "Why dost thou not join the party that drives over to see the wonders of Aladdin's Palace to-day? It would seem more proper that thou shouldst accompany thy guests than Raymond and Amita."

"I have never entered his doors since the day he was disrespectful to my mother's daughter," said Maruja, in surprise.

"Disrespectful!" repeated Dona Maria, impatiently. "Thy father's daughter ought to know that such as he may be ignorant and vulgar, but can not be disrespectful to her. And there are offenses, child, it is much more crushing to forget than to remember. As long as he has not the presumption to APOLOGIZE, I see no reason why thou mayst not go. He has not been here since that affair of the letters. I shall not permit him to be uncivil over THAT—dost thou understand? He is of use to me in business. Thou mayst take Carroll with thee; he will understand that."

"But Carroll will not go," said Maruja. "He will not say what passed between them, but I suspect they quarreled."

"All the better, then, that thou goest alone. He need not be reminded of it. Fear not but that he will be only too proud of thy visit to think of aught else."

Maruja, who seemed relieved at this prospect of being unaccompanied by Captain Carroll, shrugged her shoulders and assented.

When the party that afternoon drove into the courtyard of Aladdin's Palace, the announcement that its hospitable proprietor was absent, and would not return until dinner, did not abate either their pleasure or their curiosity. As already intimated to the reader, Mr. Prince's functions as host were characteristically irregular; and the servant's suggestion, that Mr. Prince's private secretary would attend to do the honors, created little interest, and was laughingly waived by Maruja. "There really is not the slightest necessity to trouble the gentleman," she said, politely. "I know the house thoroughly, and I think I have shown it once or twice before for your master. Indeed," she added, turning to her party, "I have been already complimented on my skill as a cicerone." After a pause, she continued, with a slight exaggeration of action and in her deepest contralto, "Ahem, ladies and gentlemen, the ball and court in which we are now standing is a perfect copy of the Court of Lions at the Alhambra, and was finished in fourteen days in white pine, gold, and plaster, at a cost of ten thousand dollars. A photograph of the original structure hangs on the wall: you will observe, ladies and gentlemen, that the reproduction is perfect. The Alhambra is in Granada, a province of Spain, which it is said in some respects to resemble California, where you have probably observed the Spanish language is still spoken by the old settlers. We now cross the stable-yard on a bridge which is a facsimile in appearance and dimensions of the Bridge of Sighs at Venice, connecting the Doge's Palace with the State Prison. Here, on the contrary, instead of being ushered into a dreary dungeon, as in the great original, a fresh surprise awaits us. Allow me, ladies and gentlemen, to precede you for the surprise. We open a door thus—and—presto!"—

She stopped, speechless, on the threshold; the fan fell from her gesticulating hand.

In the centre of a brilliantly-lit conservatory, with golden columns, a young man was standing. As her fan dropped on the tessellated pavement, he came forward, picked it up, and put it in her rigid and mechanical fingers. The party, who had applauded her apparently artistic climax, laughingly pushed by her into the conservatory, without noticing her agitation.

It was the same face and figure she remembered as last standing before her, holding back the crowding grain in the San Antonio field. But here he was appareled and appointed like a gentleman, and even seemed to be superior to the garish glitter of his new surroundings.

"I believe I have the pleasure of speaking to Miss Saltonstall," he said, with the faintest suggestion of his former manner in his half-resentful sidelong glance. "I hear that you offered to dispense with my services, but I knew that Mr. Prince would scarcely be satisfied if I did not urge it once more upon you in person. I am his private secretary."

At the same moment, Amita and Raymond, attracted by the conversation, turned towards him. Their recognition of the man they had seen at Dr. West's was equally distinct. The silence became embarrassing. Two pretty girls of the party pressed to Amita's side, with half-audible whispers. "What is it?" "Who's your handsome and wicked-looking friend?" "Is this the surprise?"

At the sound of their voices, Maruja recovered herself coldly. "Ladies," she said, with a slight wave of her fan, "this is Mr. Prince's private secretary. I believe it is hardly fair to take up his valuable time. Allow me to thank you, sir, FOR PICKING UP MY FAN."

With a single subtle flash of the eye she swept by him, taking her companions to the other end of the conservatory. When she turned, he was gone.

"This was certainly an unexpected climax," said Raymond,

mischievously. "Did you really arrange it beforehand? We leave a picturesque tramp at the edge of a grave; we pass over six weeks and a Bridge of Sighs, and hey, presto! we find a private secretary in a conservatory! This is quite the regular Aladdin business."

"You may laugh," said Maruja, who had recovered her spirits, "but if you were really clever you'd find out what it all means. Don't you see that Amita is dying of curiosity?"

"Let us fly at once and discover the secret, then," said Raymond, slipping Amita's arm through his. "We will consult the oracle in the stables. Come."

The others followed, leaving Maruja for an instant alone. She was about to rejoin them when she heard footsteps in the passage they had just crossed, and then perceived that the young stranger had merely withdrawn to allow the party to precede him before he returned to the other building through the conservatory, which he was just entering. In turning quickly to escape, the black lace of her over-skirt caught in the spines of a snaky-looking cactus. She stopped to disengage herself with feverish haste in vain. She was about to sacrifice the delicate material, in her impatience, when the young man stepped quietly to her side.

"Allow me. Perhaps I have more patience, even if I have less time," he said, stooping down. Their ungloved hands touched. Maruja stopped in her efforts and stood up. He continued until he had freed the luckless flounce, conscious of the soft fire of her eyes on his head and neck.

"There," he said, rising, and encountering her glance. As she did not speak, he continued: "You are thinking, Miss Saltonstall, that you have seen me before, are you not? Well—you HAVE; I asked you the road to San Jose one morning when I was tramping by your hedge."

"And as you probably were looking for something better—which you seem to have found—you didn't care to listen to MY directions," said Maruja, quickly.

"I found a man—almost the only one who ever offered me a gratuitous kindness—at whose grave I afterwards met you. I found another man who befriended me here—where I meet you again."

She was beginning to be hysterically nervous lest any one should return and find them together. She was conscious of a tingling of vague shame. Yet she lingered. The strange fascination of his half-savage melancholy, and a reproach-fulness that seemed to arraign her, with the rest of the world, at the bar of his vague resentment, held the delicate fibres of her sensitive being as cruelly and relentlessly as the thorns of the cactus had gripped her silken lace. Without knowing what she was saying, she stammered that she "was glad he connected her with his better fortune," and began to move away. He noticed it with his sidelong lids, and added, with a slight bitterness:—

"I don't think I should have intruded here again, but I thought you had gone. But I—I—am afraid you have not seen the last of me. It was the intention of my employer, Mr. Prince, to introduce me to you and your mother. I suppose he considers it part of my duties here. I must warn you that, if you are here when he returns, he will insist upon it, and upon your meeting me with these ladies at dinner."

"Perhaps so—he is my mother's friend," said Maruja; "but you have the advantage of us—you can always take to the road, you know."

The smile with which she had intended to accompany this speech did not come as readily in execution as it had in conception, and she would have given worlds to have recalled her words. But he said, "That's so," quietly, and turned away, as if to give her an opportunity to escape. She moved hesitatingly towards the passage and stopped. The sound of the returning voices gave her a sudden courage.

"Mr.—"

"Guest," said the young man.

"If we do conclude to stay to dinner as Mr. Prince has said nothing of introducing you to my sister, you must let ME have that pleasure."

He lifted his eyes to hers with a sudden flush. But she had fled.

She reached her party, displaying her torn flounce as the cause of her delay, and there was a slight quickness in her breathing and her speech which was attributed to the same grave reason. "But, only listen," said Amita, "we've got it all out of the butler and the grooms. It's such a romantic story!"

"What is?" said Maruja, suddenly.

"Why, the private tramp's."

"The peripatetic secretary," suggested Raymond.

"Yes," continued Amita, "Mr. Prince was so struck with his gratitude to the old Doctor that he hunted him up in San Jose, and brought him here. Since then Prince has been so interested in him—it appears he was somebody in the States, or has rich relations—that he has been telegraphing and making all sorts of inquiries about him, and has even sent out his own lawyer to hunt up everything about him. Are you listening?"

"Yes."

"You seem abstracted."

"I am hungry."

"Why not dine here; it's an hour earlier than at home. Aladdin would fall at your feet for the honor. Do!"

Maruja looked at them with innocent vagueness, as if the possibility were just beginning to dawn upon her.

"And Clara Wilson is just dying to see the mysterious unknown again. Say yes, little Maruja."

Little Maruja glanced at them with a large maternal compassion. "We shall see."

Mr. Prince, on his return an hour later, was unexpectedly delighted with Maruja's gracious acceptance of his invitation to dinner. He was thoroughly sensible of the significance which his neighbors had attached to the avoidance by the Saltonstall heiress of his various parties and gorgeous festivities ever since a certain act of indiscretion—now alleged to have been produced by the exaltation of wine—had placed him under ban. Whatever his feelings were towards her mother, he could not fail to appreciate fully this act of the daughter, which rehabilitated him. It was with more than his usual extravagance—shown even in a certain exaggeration of respect towards Maruja—that he welcomed the party, and made preparations for the dinner. The telegraph and mounted messengers were put into rapid requisition. The bridal suite was placed at the disposal of the young ladies for a dressing-room. The attendant genii surpassed themselves. The evening dresses of Maruja, Amita, and the Misses Wilson, summoned by electricity from La Mision Perdida, and dispatched by the fleetest conveyances, were placed in the arms of their maids, smothered with bouquets, an hour before dinner. An operatic concert troupe, passing through the nearest town, were diverted from their course by the slaves of the ring to discourse hidden music in the music-room during dinner. "Bite my finger, Sweetlips," said Miss Clara Wilson, who had a neat taste for apt quotation, to Maruja, "that I may see if I am awake. It's the Arabian Nights all over again!"

The dinner was a marvel, even in a land of gastronomic marvels; the dessert a miracle of fruits, even in a climate that bore the products of two zones. Maruja, from her seat beside her satisfied host, looked across a bank of yellow roses at her sister and Raymond, and was timidly conscious of the eyes of young Guest, who was seated at the other end of the table, between the two Misses Wilson. With a strange haunting of his appearance on the day she first met him, she stole glances of half-frightened curiosity at him while he was eating, and was relieved to find that he used his knife and fork like the others, and that his appetite was far from voracious. It was his employer who was the first to recall the experiences of his past life, with a certain enthusiasm and the air of a host anxious to contribute to the entertainment of his guests. "You'd hardly believe, Miss Saltonstall, that that young gentleman over there walked across the Continent—and two thousand odd miles, wasn't it?—all alone, and with not much more in the way of traps than he's got on now. Tell 'em, Harry, how the Apaches nearly gobbled you up, and then let you go because they thought you as good an Injun as any one of them, and how you lived a week in the desert on two biscuits as big as that." A chorus of entreaty and delighted anticipation followed the suggestion. The old expression of being at bay returned for an instant to Guest's face, but, lifting his eyes, he caught a look of almost sympathetic anxiety from Maruja's, who had not spoken.

"It became necessary for me, some time ago," said Guest, half explanatorily, to Maruja, "to be rather explicit in the details of my journey here, and I told Mr. Prince some things which he seems to think interesting to others. That is all. To save my life on one occasion, I was obliged to show myself as good as an Indian, in his own way, and I lived among them and traveled with them for two weeks. I have been hungry, as I suppose others have on like occasions, but nothing more."

Nevertheless, in spite of his evident reticence, he was obliged to give way to their entreaties, and, with a certain grim and uncompromising truthfulness of statement, recounted some episodes of his journey. It was none the less thrilling that he did it reluctantly, and in much the same manner as he had answered his father's questions, and as he had probably responded to the later cross-examination of Mr. Prince. He did not tell it emotionally, but rather with the dogged air of one who had been subjected to a personal grievance for which he neither asked nor expected sympathy. When he did not raise his eyes to Maruja's, he kept them fixed on his plate.

"Well," said Prince, when a long-drawn sigh of suspended emotion among the guests testified to his powers as a caterer to their amusement, "what do you say to some music with our coffee to follow the story?"

"It's more like a play," said Amita to Raymond. "What a pity Captain Carroll, who knows all about Indians, isn't here to have enjoyed it. But I suppose Maruja, who hasn't lost a word, will tell it to him."

"I don't think she will," said Raymond, dryly, glancing at Maruja, who, lost in some intricate pattern of her Chinese plate, was apparently unconscious that her host was waiting her signal to withdraw.

At last she raised her head, and said, gently but audibly, to the waiting Prince,—

"It is positively a newer pattern; the old one had not that delicate straw line in the arabesque. You must have had it made for you."

"I did," said the gratified Prince, taking up the plate. "What eyes you have, Miss Saltonstall. They see everything."

"Except that I'm keeping you all waiting," she returned, with a smile, letting the eyes in question fall with a half-parting salutation on Guest as she rose. It was the first exchange of a common instinct between them, and left them as conscious as if they had pressed hands.

The music gave an opportunity for some desultory conversation, in which Mr. Prince and his young friend received an invitation from Maruja to visit La Mision, and the party, by common consent, turned into the conservatory, where the genial host begged them each to select a flower from a few especially rare exotics. When Maruja received hers, she said, laughingly, to Prince, "Will you think me very importunate if I ask for another?" "Take what you like—you have only to name it," he replied, gallantly. "But that's just what I can't do," responded the young girl, "unless," she added, turning to Guest, "unless you can assist me. It was the plant I was examining to-day." "I think I can show it to you," said Guest, with a slight increase of color, as he preceded her towards the memorable cactus near the door, "but I doubt if it has any flower."

Nevertheless, it had. A bright red blossom, like a spot of blood drawn by one of its thorns. He plucked it for her, and she placed it in her belt.

"You are forgiving," he said, admiringly.

"YOU ought to know that," she returned, looking down.

"I?—why?"

"You were rude to me twice."

"Twice!"

"Yes—once at the Mision of La Perdida; once in the road at San Antonio."

His eyes became downcast and gloomy. "At the Mision that morning, I, a wretched outcast, only saw in you a beautiful girl intent on overriding me with her merciless beauty. At San Antonio I handed the fan I picked up to the man whose eyes told me he loved you."

She started impatiently. "You might have been more gallant, and found more difficulty in the selection," she said, pertly. "But since when have you gentlemen become so observant and so punctilious? Would you expect him to be as considerate of others?"

"I have few claims that any one seems bound to respect," he returned, brusquely. Then, in a softer voice, he added, looking at her, gently,—

"You were in mourning when you came here this afternoon, Miss Saltonstall."

"Was I? It was for Dr. West—my mother's friend."

"It was very becoming to you."

"You are complimenting me. But I warn you that Captain Carroll said something better than that; he said mourning was not necessary for me. I had only to 'put my eye-lashes at half-mast.' He is a soldier you know."

"He seems to be as witty as he is fortunate," said Guest, bitterly.

"Do you think he is fortunate?" said Maruja, raising her eyes to his. There was so much in this apparently simple question that Guest looked in her eyes for a suggestion. What he saw there for an instant made his heart stop beating. She apparently did not know it, for she began to tremble too.

"Is he not?" said Guest, in a low voice.

"Do you think he ought to be?" she found herself whispering.

A sudden silence fell upon them. The voices of their companions seemed very far in the distance; the warm breath of the flowers appeared to be drowning their senses; they tried to speak, but could not; they were so near to each other that the two long blades of a palm served to hide them. In the midst of this profound silence a voice that was like and yet unlike Maruja's said twice, "Go! go!" but each time seemed hushed in the stifling silence. The next moment the palms were pushed aside, the dark figure of a young man slipped like some lithe animal through the shrubbery, and Maruja found herself standing, pale and rigid, in the middle of the walk, in the full glare of the light, and looking down the corridor toward her approaching companions. She was furious and frightened; she was triumphant and trembling; without thought, sense, or reason, she had been kissed by Henry Guest, and—had returned it.

The fleetest horses of Aladdin's stud that night could not carry her far enough or fast enough to take her away from that moment, that scene, and that sensation. Wise and experienced, confident in her beauty, secure in her selfishness, strong over others' weaknesses, weighing accurately the deeds and words of men and women, recognizing all there was in position and tradition, seeing with her father's clear eyes the practical meaning of any divergence from that conventionality which as a woman of the world she valued, she returned again and again to the trembling joy of that intoxicating moment. She though of her mother and sisters, of Raymond and Garnier, of Aladdin— she even forced herself to think of Carroll—only to shut her eyes, with a faint smile, and dream again the brief but thrilling dream of Guest that began and ended in their joined and parted lips. Small wonder that, hidden and silent in her enwrappings, as she lay back in the carriage, with her pale face against the cold starry sky, two other stars came out and glistened and trembled on her passion-fringed lashes.

CHAPTER X

The rainy season had set in early. The last three weeks of summer drought had drained the great valley of its lifeblood; the dead stalks of grain rustled like dry bones over Dr. West's grave. The desiccating wind and sun had wrought some disenchanting cracks and fissures in Aladdin's Palace, and otherwise disjoined it, so that it not only looked as if it were ready to be packed away, but had become finally untenable in the furious onset of the southwesterly rains. The gorgeous furniture of the reception-rooms was wrapped in mackintoshes, the conservatory was changed into an aquarium, the Bridge of Sighs crossed an actual canal in the stable-yard. Only the billiard-room and Mr. Prince's bedroom and office remained intact, and in the latter, one stormy afternoon, Mr. Prince himself sat busy over his books and papers. His station-wagon, splashed and streaked with mud, stood in the court-yard, just as it had been driven from the station, and the smell of the smoke of newly-lit fires showed that the house had been opened only for this hurried visit of its owner.

The tramping of horse hoofs in the court-yard was soon followed by steps along the corridor, and the servant ushered Captain Carroll into the presence of his master. The Captain did not remove his military overcoat, but remained standing erect in the centre of the room, with his forage cap in his hand.

"I could have given you a lift from the station," said Prince, "if you had come that way. I've only just got in myself."

"I preferred to ride," said Carroll, dryly.

"Sit down by the fire," said Prince, motioning to a chair, "and dry yourself."

"I must ask you first the purport of this interview," said Carroll, curtly, "before I prolong it further. You have asked me to come here in reference to certain letters I returned to their rightful owner some months ago. If you seek to reclaim them again, or to refer to a subject which must remain forgotten, I decline to proceed further."

"It DOES refer to the letters, and it rests with you whether they shall be forgotten or not. It is not my fault if the subject has been dropped. You must remember that until yesterday you have been absent on a tour of inspection and could not be applied to before."

Carroll cast a cold glance at Prince, and then threw himself into a chair, with his overcoat still on and his long military boots crossed before the fire. Sitting there in profile Prince could not but notice that he looked older and sterner than at their last interview, and his cheeks were thinned as if by something more than active service.

"When you were here last summer," began Prince, leaning forward over his desk, "you brought me a piece of news that astounded me, as it did many others. It was the assignment of Dr. West's property to Mrs. Saltonstall. That was something there was no gainsaying; it was a purely business affair, and involved nobody's rights but the assignor. But this was followed, a day or two after, by the announcement of the Doctor's will, making the same lady the absolute and sole inheritor of the same property. That seemed all right too; for there were, apparently, no legal heirs. Since then, however, it has been discovered that there is a legal heir—none other than the Doctor's only son. Now, as no allusion to the son's existence was made in that will—which was a great oversight of the Doctor's—it is a fiction of the law that such an omission is an act of forgetfulness, and therefore leaves the son the same rights as if there had been no will at all. In other words, if the Doctor had seen fit to throw his scapegrace son a hundred dollar bill, it would have been legal evidence that he remembered him. As he did not, it's a fair legal presumption that he forgot him, or that the will is incomplete."

"This seems to be a question for Mrs. Saltonstall's lawyers—not for her friends," said Carroll, coldly.

"Excuse me; that remains for you to decide—when you hear all. You understand at present, then, that Dr. West's property, both by assignment and will, was made over, in the event of his death, not to his legal heirs, but to a comparative stranger. It looked queer to a good many people, but the only explanation was, that the Doctor had fallen very much in love with the widow—that he would have probably married her—had he lived."

With an unpleasant recollection that this was almost exactly Maruja's explanation of her mother's relations to Dr. West, Carroll returned, impatiently, "If you mean that their private relations may be made the subject of legal discussion, in the event of litigation in regard to the property, that again is a matter for Mrs. Saltonstall to decide—and not her friends. It is purely a matter of taste."

"It may be a matter of discretion, Captain Carroll."

"Of discretion!" repeated Carroll, superciliously.

"Well," said Prince, leaving his desk and coming to the fire-place, with his hands in his pockets, "what would you call it, if it could be found that Dr. West, on leaving Mrs. Saltonstall's that night, did not meet with an accident, was not thrown from his horse, but was coolly and deliberately murdered!"

Captain Carroll's swift recollection of the discovery he himself had made in the road, and its inconsistency with the accepted theory of the accident, unmistakably showed itself in his face. It was a moment before he recovered himself.

"But even if it can be proved to have been a murder and not an accident, what has that to do with Mrs. Saltonstall or her claim to the property?"

"Only that she was the one person directly benefited by his death."

Captain Carroll looked at him steadily, and then rose to his feet. "Do I understand that you have called me here to listen to this infamous aspersion of a lady?"

"I have called you here, Captain Carroll, to listen to the arguments that may be used to set aside Dr. West's will, and return the property to the legal heir. You are to listen to them or not, as you choose; but I warn you that your opportunity to hear them in confidence and convey them to your friend will end here. I have no opinion in the case. I only tell you that it will be argued that Dr. West was unduly influenced to make a will in Mrs. Saltonstall's favor; that, after having done so, it will be shown that, just before his death, he became aware of the existence of his son and heir, and actually had an interview with him; that he visited Mrs. Saltonstall that evening, with the records of his son's identity and a memorandum of his interview in his pocket-book; and that, an hour after leaving the house, he was foully murdered. That is the theory which Mrs. Saltonstall has to consider. I told you I have no opinion. I only know that there are witnesses to the interview of the Doctor and his son; there is evidence of murder, and the murderer is suspected; there is the evidence of the pocket-book, with the memorandum picked up on the spot, which you handed me yourself."

"Do you mean to say that you will permit this pocketbook, handed you in confidence, to be used for such an infamous purpose?" said Carroll.

"I think you offered it to me in exchange for Dr. West's letters to Mrs. Saltonstall," returned Prince, dryly. "The less said about that, the less is likely to be said about compromising letters written by the widow to the Doctor, which she got you to recover—letters which they may claim had a bearing on the case, and even lured him to his fate."

For an instant Captain Carroll recoiled before the gulf which seemed to open at the feet of the unhappy family. For an instant a terrible doubt possessed him, and in that doubt he found a new reason for a certain changed and altered tone in Maruja's later correspondence with him, and the vague hints she had thrown out of the impossibility of their union. "I beg you will not press me to greater candor," she had written, "and try to forget me before you learn to hate me." For an instant he believed—and even took a miserable comfort in the belief—that it was this hideous secret, and not some coquettish caprice, to which she vaguely alluded. But it was only for a moment; the next instant the monstrous doubt passed from the mind of the simple gentleman, with only a slight flush of shame at his momentary disloyalty.

Prince, however, had noticed it, not without a faint sense of sympathy. "Look here!" he said, with a certain brusqueness, which in a man of his character was less dangerous than his smoothness. "I know your feelings to that family—at least to one of them—and, if I've been playing it pretty rough on you, it's only because you played it rather rough on ME the last time you were here. Let's understand each other. I'll go so far as to say I don't believe that Mrs. Saltonstall had anything to do with that murder, but, as a business man, I'm bound to say that these circumstances and her own indiscretion are quite enough to bring the biggest pressure down on her. I wouldn't want any better 'bear' on the market value of her rights than this. Take it at its best. Say that the Coroner's verdict is set aside, and a charge of murder against unknown parties is made—"

"One moment, Mr. Prince," said Carroll. "I shall be one of the first to insist that this is done, and I have confidence enough in Mrs. Saltonstall's honest friendship for the Doctor to know that she will lose no time in pursuing his murderers."

Prince looked at Carroll with a feeling of half envy and half pity. "I think not," he said, dryly; "for all suspicion points to one man as the perpetrator, and that man was Mrs. Saltonstall's confidential servant—the mayordomo, Pereo." He waited for a moment for the effect of this announcement on Carroll, and then went on: "You now understand that, even if Mrs. Saltonstall is acquitted of any connivance with or even knowledge of the deed, she will hardly enjoy the prosecution of her confidential servant for murder."

"But how can this be prevented? If, as you say, there are actual proofs, why have they not been acted upon before?

What can keep them from being acted upon now?"

"The proofs have been collected by one man, have been in possession of one man, and will only pass out of his possession when it is for the benefit of the legal heir—who does not yet even know of their existence."

"And who is this one man?"

"Myself."

"You?—You?" said Carroll, advancing towards him. "Then this is YOUR work!"

"Captain Carroll," said Prince, without moving, but drawing his lips tightly together and putting his head on one side, "I don't propose to have another scene like the one we had at our last meeting. If you try on anything of that kind, I shall put the whole matter into a lawyer's hands. I don't say that you won't regret it; I don't say that I sha'nt be disappointed, too, for I have been managing this thing purely as a matter of business, with a view to profiting by it. It so happens that we can both work to the same end, even if our motives are not the same. I don't call myself an officer and a gentleman, but I reckon I've run this affair about as delicately as the best of them, and with a d—d sight more horse sense. I want this thing hushed up and compromised, to get some control of the property again, and to prevent it depreciating, as it would, in litigation; you want it hushed up for the sake of the girl and your future mother-in-law. I don't know anything about your laws of honor, but I've laid my cards on the table for you to see, without asking what you've got in your hand. You can play the game or leave the board, as you choose." He turned and walked to the window—not without leaving on Carroll's mind a certain sense of firmness, truthfulness, and sincerity which commanded his respect.

"I withdraw any remark that might have seemed to reflect on your business integrity, Mr. Prince," said Carroll, quietly. "I am willing to admit that you have managed this thing better than I could, and, if I join you in an act to suppress these revelations, I have no right to judge of your intentions. What do you propose to have me do?"

"To state the whole case to Mrs. Saltonstall, and to ask her to acknowledge the young man's legal claim without litigation."

"But how do you know that she would not do this without—excuse me—without intimidation?"

"I only reckon that a woman clever enough to get hold of a million, would be clever enough to keep it—against others."

"I hope to show you are mistaken. But where is this heir?"

"Here."

"Here?"

"Yes. For the last six months he has been my private secretary. I know what you are thinking of, Captain Carroll. You would consider it indelicate—eh? Well, that's just where we differ. By this means I have kept everything in my own hands—prevented him from getting into the hands of outsiders—and I intend to dispose of just as much of the facts to him as may be necessary for him to prove his title. What bargain I make with HIM—is my affair."

"Does he suspect the murder?"

"No. I did not think it necessary for his good or mine. He can be an ugly devil if he likes, and although there wasn't much love lost between him and the old man, it wouldn't pay to have any revenge mixed up with business. He knows nothing of it. It was only by accident that, looking after his movements while he was here, I ran across the tracks of the murderer."

"But what has kept him from making known his claim to the Saltonstalls? Are you sure he has not?" said Carroll, with a sudden thought that it might account for Maruja's strangeness.

"Positive. He's too proud to make a claim unless he could thoroughly prove it, and only a month ago he made me promise to keep it dark. He's too lazy to trouble himself about it much anyway—as far as I can see. D—d if I don't think his being a tramp has made him lose his taste for everything! Don't worry yourself about HIM. He isn't likely to make confidences with the Saltonstalls, for he don't like 'em, and never went there but once. Instinctively or not, the widow didn't cotton to him; and I fancy Miss Maruja has some old grudge against him for that fan business on the road. She isn't a girl to forgive or forget anything, as I happen to know," he added, with an uneasy laugh.

Carroll was too preoccupied with the danger that seemed to threaten his friends from this surly pretender to resent Prince's tactless allusion. He was thinking of Maruja's ominous agitation at his presence at Dr. West's grave. "Do they suspect him at all?"—he asked, hurriedly.

"How should they? He goes by the name of Guest—which was his father's real name until changed by an act of legislation when he first came here. Nobody remembers it. We only found it out from his papers. It was quite legal, as all his property was acquired under the name of West."

Carroll rose and buttoned his overcoat. "I presume you are

able to offer conclusive proofs of everything you have asserted?"

"Perfectly."

"I am going to the Mision Perdida now," said Captain Carroll, quietly. "To-morrow I will bring you the answer— Peace or War." He walked to the door, lifted his hand to his cap, with a brief military salutation, and disappeared.

CHAPTER XI

As Captain Carroll urged his horse along the miry road to La Mision Perdida, he was struck with certain changes in the landscape before him other than those wrought by the winter rains. There were the usual deep gullies and trenches, half-filled with water, in the fields and along the road, but there were ominous embankments and ridges of freshly turned soil, and a scattered fringe of timbers following a cruel, undeviating furrow on the broad grazing lands of the Mision. But it was not until he had crossed the arroyo that he felt the full extent of the late improvements. A quick rumbling in the distance, a light flash of steam above the willow copse, that drifted across the field on his right, and he knew that the railroad was already in operation. Captain Carroll reined in his frightened charger, and passed his hand across his brow with a dazed sense of loss. He had been gone only four months—yet he already felt strange and forgotten.

It was with a feeling of relief that he at last turned from the high-road into the lane. Here everything was unchanged, except that the ditches were more thickly strewn with the sodden leaves of fringing oaks and sycamores. Giving his horse to a servant in the court-yard, he did not enter the patio, but, crossing the lawn, stepped upon the long veranda. The rain was dripping from its eaves and striking a minute spray from the vines that clung to its columns; his footfall awoke a hollow echo as he passed, as if the outer shell of the house were deserted; the formal yews and hemlocks that in summer had relieved the dazzling glare of six months' sunshine had now taken gloomy possession of the garden, and the evening shadows, thickened by rain, seemed to lie in wait at every corner. The servant, who had, with old-fashioned courtesy, placed the keys and the "disposition" of that wing of the house at his service, said that Dona Maria would wait upon him in the salon before dinner. Knowing the difficulty of breaking the usual rigid etiquette, and trusting to the happy intervention of Maruja—though here, again, custom debarred him from asking for her—he allowed the servant to remove his wet overcoat, and followed him to the stately and solemn chamber prepared for him. The silence and gloom of the great house, so grateful and impressive in the ardent summer, began to weigh upon him under this shadow of an overcast sky. He walked to the window and gazed out on the cloister-like veranda. A melancholy willow at an angle of the stables seemed to be wringing its hands in the rising wind. He turned for relief to the dim fire that flickered like a votive taper in the vault-like hearth, and drew a chair towards it. In spite of the impatience and preoccupation of a lover, he found himself again and again recurring to the story he had just heard, until the vengeful spirit of the murdered Doctor seemed to darken and possess the house. He was striving to shake off the feeling, when his attention was attracted to stealthy footsteps in the passage. Could it be Maruja? He rose to his feet, with his eye upon the door. The footsteps ceased—it remained closed. But another door, which had escaped his attention in the darkened corner, slowly swung on its hinges, and, with a stealthy step, Pereo, the mayordomo, entered the room.

Courageous and self-possessed as Captain Carroll was by nature and education, this malevolent vision, and incarnation of the thought uppermost in his mind, turned him cold. He had half drawn a derringer from his breast, when his eye fell on the grizzled locks and wrinkled face of the old man, and his hand dropped to his side. But Pereo, with the quick observation of insanity, had noticed the weapon, and rubbed his hands together, with a malicious laugh.

"Good! good! good!" he whispered, rapidly, in a strange bodiless voice; "'t will serve! 't will serve! And you are a soldier too—and know how to use it! Good, it is a Providence!" He lifted his hollow eyes to heaven, and then added, "Come! come!"

Carroll stepped towards him. He was alone and in the presence of an undoubted madman—one strong enough, in spite of his years, to inflict a deadly injury, and one whom he now began to realize might have done so once before. Nevertheless, he laid his hand on the old man's arm, and, looking him calmly in the eye, said, quietly, "Come? Where, Pereo? I have only just arrived."

"I know it," whispered the old man, nodding his head violently. "I was watching them, when you rode up. That is why I lost the scent; but together we can track them still—we can track them. Eh, Captain, eh! Come! Come!" and he moved slowly backward, waving his hand towards the door.

"Track whom, Pereo?" said Carroll, soothingly. "Whom do you seek?"

"Whom?" said the old man, startled for a moment and passing his hand over his wrinkled forehead. "Whom? Eh! Why, the Dona Maruja and the little black cat—her maid—Faquita!"

"Yes, but why seek them? Why track them?"

"Why?" said the old man, with a sudden burst of impotent passion. "YOU ask me why! Because they are going to the rendezvous again. They are going to seek him. Do you understand—to seek HIM—the Coyote!"

Carroll smiled a faint smile of relief—"So—the Coyote!"

"Ay," said the old man, in a confidential whisper; "the Coyote! But not the big one—you understand—the little one. The big one is dead—dead—dead! But the little one lives yet. You shall do for HIM what I, Pereo—listen—" he glanced around the room furtively—"what I—the good old Pereo, did for the big one! Good, it is a Providence. Come!"

Of the terrible thoughts that crossed Carroll's mind at this unexpected climax one alone was uppermost. The trembling irresponsible wretch before him meditated some vague crime—and Maruja was in danger. He did not allow himself to dwell upon any other suspicion suggested by that speech; he quickly conceived a plan of action. To have rung the bell and given Pereo into the hands of the servants would have only exposed to them the lunatic's secret—if he had any— and he might either escape in his fury or relapse into useless imbecility. To humor him and follow him, and trust afterwards to his own quickness and courage to avert any calamity, seemed to be the only plan. Captain Carroll turned his clear glance on the restless eyes of Pereo, and said, without emotion, "Let us go, then, and quickly. You shall track them for me; but remember, good Pereo, you must leave the rest to me."

In spite of himself, some accidental significance in this ostentatious adjuration to lull Pereo's suspicions struck him with pain. But the old man's eyes glittered with gratified passion as he said, "Ay, good! I will keep my word. Thou shalt work thy will on the little one as I have said. Truly it is a Providence! Come!" Seeing Captain Carroll glance round for his overcoat, he seized a poncho from the wall, wrapped it round him, and grasped his hand. Carroll, who would have evaded this semblance of disguise, had no time to parley, and they turned together, through the door by which Pereo had entered, into a long dark passage, which seemed to be made through the outer shell of the building that flanked the park. Following his guide in the profound obscurity, perfectly conscious that any change in his madness might be followed by a struggle in the dark, where no help could reach them, they presently came to a door that opened upon the fresh smell of rain and leaves. They were standing at the bottom of a secluded alley, between two high hedges that hid it from the end of the garden. Its grass-grown walk and untrimmed hedges showed that it was seldom used. Carroll, still keeping close to Pereo's side, felt him suddenly stop and tremble. "Look!" he said, pointing to a shadowy figure some distance before them; "look, 'tis Maruja, and alone!"

With a dexterous movement, Carroll managed to slip his arm securely through the old man's, and even to throw himself before him, as if in his eagerness to discern the figure.

"'Tis Maruja—and alone!" said Pereo, trembling. "Alone! Eh! And the Coyote is not here!" He passed his hand over his staring eyes. "So." Suddenly he turned upon Carroll. "Ah, do you not see, it is a trick! The Coyote is escaping with Faquita! Come! Nay; thou wilt not? Then will I!" With an unexpected strength born of his madness, he freed his arm from Carroll and darted down the alley. The figure of Maruja, evidently alarmed at his approach, glided into the hedge, as Pereo passed swiftly by, intent only on his one wild fancy. Without a further thought of his companion or even the luckless Faquita, Carroll also plunged through the hedge, to intercept Maruja. But by that time she was already crossing the upper end of the lawn, hurrying towards the entrance to the patio. Carroll did not hesitate to follow. Keeping in view the lithe, dark, active little figure, now hidden by an intervening cluster of bushes, now fading in the gathering evening shadows, he nevertheless did not succeed in gaining upon her until she had nearly reached the patio. Here he lost ground, as turning to the right, instead of entering the court-yard, she kept her way toward the stables. He was near enough, however, to speak. "One moment, Miss Saltonstall," he said hurriedly; "there is no danger. I am alone. But I must speak with you."

The young girl seemed only to redouble her exertions. At last she stopped before a narrow door hidden in the wall, and fumbled in her pocket for a key. That moment Carroll was upon her.

"Forgive me, Miss Saltonstall—Maruja; but you must hear me! You are safe, but I fear for your maid, Faquita!"

A little laugh followed his speech; the door yielded and opened to her vanishing figure. For an instant the lace shawl muffling her face was lifted, as the door closed and locked behind her. Carroll drew back in consternation. It was the laughing eyes and saucy face of Faquita!

CHAPTER XII

When Captain Carroll turned from the high-road into the lane, an hour before, Maruja and Faquita had already left the house by the same secret passage and garden-door that opened afterwards upon himself and Pereo. The young women had evidently changed dresses: Maruja was wearing the costume of her maid; Faquita was closely veiled and habited like her mistress; but it was characteristic that, while Faquita appeared awkward and over-dressed in her borrowed plumes, Maruja's short saya and trim bodice, with the striped shawl that hid her fair head, looked infinitely more coquettish and bewitching than on its legitimate owner.

They passed hurriedly down the long alley, and at its further end turned at right angles to a small gate half hidden in the shrubbery. It opened upon a venerable vineyard, that dated back to the occupation of the padres, but was now given over to the chance cultivation of peons and domestics. Its long, broken rows of low vines, knotted and overgrown with age, reached to the thicketed hillside of buckeye that marked the beginning of the canada. Here Maruja parted from her maid, and, muffling the shawl more closely round her head, hastily passed between the vine rows to a ruined adobe building near the hillside. It was originally part of the refectory of the old Mision, but had been more recently used as a vinadero's cottage. As she neared it, her steps grew slower, until, reaching its door, she hesitated, with her hand timidly on the latch. The next moment she opened it gently; it was closed quickly behind her, and, with a little stifled cry, she found herself in the arms of Henry Guest.

It was only for an instant; the pleading of her white hands, disengaged from his neck, where at first they had found themselves, and uplifted before her face, touched him more than the petitioning eyes or the sweet voiceless mouth, whose breath even was forgotten. Letting her sink into the chair from which he had just risen, he drew back a step, with his hands clasped before him, and his dark half-savage eyes bent earnestly upon her. Well might he have gazed. It was no longer the conscious beauty, proud and regnant, seated before him; but a timid, frightened girl, struggling with her first deep passion.

All that was wise and gentle that she had intended to say, all that her clear intellect and experience had taught her, died upon her lips with that kiss. And all that she could do of womanly dignity and high-bred decorum was to tuck her small feet under her chair, in the desperate attempt to lengthen her short skirt, and beg him not to look at her.

"I have had to change dresses with Faquita, because we were watched," she said, leaning forward in her chair and drawing the striped shawl around her shoulders. "I have had to steal out of my mother's house and through the fields, as if I was a gypsy. If I only were a gypsy, Harry, and not—"

"And not the proudest heiress in the land," he interrupted, with something of his old bitterness. "True, I had forgot."

"But I never reminded you of it," she said, lifting her eyes to his. "I did not remind you of it on that day—in—in—in the conservatory, nor at the time you first spoke of—of—love to me—nor from the time I first consented to meet you here. It is YOU, Harry, who have spoken of the difference of our condition, YOU who have talked of my wealth, my family, my position—until I would gladly have changed places with Faquita as I have garments, if I had thought it would make you happier."

"Forgive me, darling!" he said, dropping on one knee before her and bending over the cold little hand he had taken, until his dark head almost rested in her lap. "Forgive me! You are too proud, Maruja, to admit, even to yourself, that you have given your heart where your hand and fortune could not follow. But others may not think so. I am proud, too, and will not have it said that I have won you before I was worthy of you."

"You have no right to be more proud than I, sir," she said, rising to her feet, with a touch of her old supreme assertion. "No—don't, Harry—please, Harry—there!" Nevertheless, she succumbed; and, when she went on, it was with her head resting on his shoulder. "It's this deceit and secrecy that is so shameful, Harry. I think I could bear everything with you, if it were all known—if you came to woo me like—like—the others. Even if they abused you—if they spoke of your doubtful origin—of your poverty—of your hardships! When they aspersed you, I could fight them; when they spoke of your having no father that you could claim, I could even lie for you, I think, Harry, and say that you had; if they spoke of your poverty, I would speak of my wealth; if they talked of your hardships, I should only be proud of your endurance— if I could only keep the tears from my eyes!" They were there now. He kissed them away.

"But if they threatened you? If they drove me from the house?"

"I should fly with you," she said, hiding her head in his breast.

"What if I were to ask you to fly with me now?" he said, gloomily.

"Now!" she repeated, lifting her frightened eyes to his.

His face darkened, with its old look of savage resentment. "Hear me, Maruja," he said, taking her hands tightly in his own. "When I forgot myself—when I was mad that day in the conservatory, the only expiation I could think of was to swear in my inmost soul that I would never take advantage of your forgiveness, that I would never tempt you to forget yourself, your friends, your family, for me, an unknown outcast. When I found you pitied me, and listened to my love—I was too weak to forego the one ray of sunshine in my wretched life—and, thinking that I had a prospect before me in an idea I promised to reveal to you later, I swore never to beguile you or myself in that hope by any act that might bring you to repent it—or myself to dishonor. But I taxed myself too much, Maruja. I have asked too much of you. You are right, darling; this secrecy—this deceit—is unworthy of us! Every hour of it—blest as it has been to me—every moment—sweet as it is—blackens the purity of our only defense, makes you false and me a coward! It must end here—to-day! Maruja, darling, my precious one! God knows what may be the success of my plans. We have but one chance now. I must leave here to-day, never to return, or I must take you with me. Do not start, Maruja—but hear me out. Dare you risk all? Dare you fly with me now, to-night, to the old Padre at the ruined Mision, and let him bind us in those bonds that none dare break? We can take Faquita with us—it is but a few miles—and we can return and throw ourselves at your mother's feet. She can only drive us forth together. Or we can fly from this cursed wealth, and all the misery it has entailed—forever."

She raised her head, and, with her two hands on his shoulders, gazed at him with her father's searching eyes, as if to read his very soul.

"Are you mad, Harry!—think what you propose! Is this not tempting me? Think again, dearest," she said, half convulsively, seizing his arm when her grasp had slipped from his shoulder.

There was a momentary silence as she stood with her eyes fixed almost wildly on his set face. But a sudden shock against the bolted door and an inarticulate outcry startled them. With an instinctive movement, Guest threw his arm round her.

"It's Pereo," she said, in a hurried whisper, but once more mistress of her strength and resolution. "He is seeking YOU! Fly at once. He is mad, Harry; a raving lunatic. He watched us the last time. He has tracked us here. He suspects you. You must not meet him. You can escape through the other door, that opens upon the canada. If you love me—fly!"

"And leave YOU exposed to his fury—are you mad! No. Fly yourself by the other door, lock it behind you, and alarm the servants. I will open this door to him, secure him here, and then be gone. Do not fear for me. There is no danger—and if I mistake not," he added, with a strange significance, "he will hardly attack me!"

"But he may have already alarmed the household. Hark!"

There was the noise of a struggle outside the door, and then the voice of Captain Carroll, calm and collected, rose clearly for an instant. "You are quite safe, Miss Saltonstall. I think I have him secure, but perhaps you had better not open the door until assistance comes."

They gazed at each other, without a word. A grim challenge played on Guest's lips. Maruja lifted her little hands deliberately, and clasped them round his defiant neck.

"Listen, darling," she said, softly and quietly, as if only the security of silence and darkness encompassed them. "You asked me just now if I would fly with you—if I would marry you, without the consent of my family—against the protest of my friends—and at once! I hesitated, Harry, for I was frightened and foolish. But I say to you now that I will marry you when and where you like—for I love you, Harry, and you alone."

"Then let us go at once," he said, passionately seizing her; "we can reach the road by the canada before assistance comes—before we are discovered. Come!"

"And you will remember in the years to come, Harry," she said, still composedly, and with her arms still around his neck, "that I never loved any but you—that I never knew what love was before, and that since I have loved you—I have never thought of any other. Will you not?"

"I will—and now—"

"And now," she said, with a superb gesture towards the barrier which separated them from Carroll, "OPEN THE DOOR!"

CHAPTER XIII

With a swift glance of admiration at Maruja, Guest flung open the door. The hastily-summoned servants were already bearing away the madman, exhausted by his efforts. Captain Carroll alone remained there, erect and motionless, before the threshold.

At a sign from Maruja, he entered the room. In the flash of light made by the opening door, he had been perfectly conscious of her companion, but not a motion of his eye or the movement of a muscle of his face betrayed it. The trained discipline of his youth stood him in good service, and for the moment left him master of the situation.

"I think no apology is needed for this intrusion," he said, with cool composure. "Pereo seemed intent on murdering somebody or something, and I followed him here. I suppose I might have got him away more quietly, but I was afraid you might have thoughtlessly opened the door." He stopped, and added, "I see now how unfounded was the supposition."

It was a fatal addition. In the next instant, the Maruja who had been standing beside Guest, conscious-stricken and remorseful in the presence of the man she had deceived, and calmly awaiting her punishment, changed at this luckless exhibition of her own peculiar womanly weapons. The old

Maruja, supreme, ready, undaunted, and passionless, returned to the fray.

"You were wrong, Captain," she said, sweetly; "fortunately, Mr. Guest—whom I see you have forgotten in your absence —was with me, and I think would have felt it his duty to have protected me. But I thank you all the same, and I think even Mr. Guest will not allow his envy of your good fortune in coming so gallantly to my rescue to prevent his appreciating its full value. I am only sorry that on your return to La Mision Perdida you should have fallen into the arms of a madman before extending your hands to your friends."

Their eyes met. She saw that he hated her—and felt relieved.

"It may not have been so entirely unfortunate," he said, with a coldness strongly in contrast with his gradually blazing eyes, "for I was charged with a message to you, in which this madman is supposed by some to play an important part."

"Is it a matter of business?" said Maruja, lightly, yet with a sudden instinctive premonition of coming evil in the relentless tones of his voice.

"It is business, Miss Saltonstall—purely and simply business," said Carroll, dryly, "under whatever OTHER name it may have been since presented to you."

"Perhaps you have no objection to tell it before Mr. Guest," said Maruja, with an inspiration of audacity; "it sounds so mysterious that it must be interesting. Otherwise, Captain Carroll, who abhors business, would not have undertaken it with more than his usual enthusiasm."

"As the business DOES interest Mr. Guest, or Mr. West, or whatever name he may have decided upon since I had the pleasure of meeting him," said Carroll—for the first time striking fire from the eyes of his rival—"I see no reason why I should not, even at the risk of telling you what you already know. Briefly, then, Mr. Prince charged me to advise you and your mother to avoid litigation with this gentleman, and admit his claim, as the son of Dr. West, to his share of the property."

The utter consternation and bewilderment shown in the face of Maruja convinced Carroll of his fatal error. She HAD received the addresses of this man without knowing his real position! The wild theory that had seemed to justify his resentment—that she had sold herself to Guest to possess the property—now recoiled upon him in its utter baseness. She had loved Guest for himself alone; by this base revelation he had helped to throw her into his arms.

But he did not even yet know Maruja. Turning to Guest, with flashing eyes, she said, "Is it true—are you the son of Dr. West, and"—she hesitated—"kept out of your inheritance by US?"

"I AM the son of Dr. West," he said, earnestly, "though I alone had the right to tell you that at the proper time and occasion. Believe me that I have given no one the right— least of all any tool of Prince—to TRADE upon it."

"Then," said Carroll, fiercely, forgetting everything in his anger, "perhaps you will disclaim before this young lady the charge made by your employer that Pereo was instigated to Dr. West's murder by her mother?"

Again he had overshot the mark. The horror and indignation depicted in Guest's face was too plainly visible to Maruja, as well as himself, to permit a doubt that the idea was as new as the accusation. Forgetting her bewilderment at these revelations, her wounded pride, a torturing doubt suggested by Guest's want of confidence in her—indeed everything but the outraged feelings of her lover, she flew to his side. "Not a word," she said, proudly, lifting her little hand before his darkening face. "Do not insult me by replying to such an accusation in my presence. Captain Carroll," she continued, turning towards him, "I cannot forget that you were introduced into my mother's house as an officer and a gentleman. When you return to it as such, and not as a MAN OF BUSINESS, you will be welcome. Until then, farewell!"

She remained standing, erect and passionless, as Carroll, with a cold salutation, stepped back and disappeared in the darkness; and then she turned, and, with tottering step and a little cry, fell upon Guest's breast. "O Harry—Harry!—why have you deceived me!"

"I thought it for the best, darling," he said, lifting her face to his. "You know now the prospect I spoke of—the hope that buoyed me up! I wanted to win you myself alone, without appealing to your sense of justice or even your sympathies! I did win you. God knows, if I had not, you would never have learned through me that a son of Dr. West had ever lived. But that was not enough. When I found that I could establish my right to my father's property, I wanted you to marry me before YOU knew it; so that it never could be said that you were influenced by anything but love for me. That was why I came here to-day. That was why I pressed you to fly with me!"

He ceased. She was fumbling with the buttons of his waistcoat. "Harry," she said, softly, "did you think of the property when—when—you kissed me in the conservatory?"

"I thought of nothing but YOU," he answered, tenderly.

Suddenly she started from his embrace. "But Pereo!—Harry—tell me quick—no one-nobody can think that this poor demented old man could—that Dr. West was—that—it's all a trick—isn't it? Harry—speak!"

He was silent for a moment, and then said, gravely, "There were strange men at the fonda that night, and—my father was supposed to carry money with him. My own life was attempted at the Mision the same evening for the sake of some paltry gold pieces that I had imprudently shown. I was saved solely by the interference of one man. That man was Pereo, your mayordomo!"

She seized his hand and raised it joyfully to her lips. "Thank you for those words! And you will come to him with me at once; and he will recognize you; and we will laugh at those lies; won't we, Harry?"

He did not reply. Perhaps he was listening to a confused sound of voices rapidly approaching the cottage. Together they stepped out into the gathering night. A number of figures were coming towards them, among them Faquita, who ran a little ahead to meet her mistress.

"Oh, Dona Maruja, he has escaped!"

"Who? Not Pereo!"

"Truly. And on his horse. It was saddled and bridled in the stable all day. One knew it not. He was walking like a cat, when suddenly he parted the peons around him, like grain before a mad bull—and behold! he was on the pinto's back and away. And, alas! there is no horse that can keep up with the pinto. God grant he may not get in the way of the r-r-railroad, that, in his very madness, he will even despise."

"My own horse is in the thicket," whispered Guest, hurriedly, in Maruja's ear. "I have measured him with the pinto before now. Give me your blessing, and I will bring him back if he be alive."

She pressed his hand and said, "Go." Before the astonished servants could identify the strange escort of their mistress, he was gone.

It was already quite dark. To any but Guest, who had made the topography of La Mision Perdida a practical study, and who had known the habitual circuit of the mayordomo in his efforts to avoid him, the search would have been hopeless. But, rightly conjecturing that he would in his demented condition follow the force of habit, he spurred his horse along the high-road until he reached the lane leading to the grassy amphitheatre already described, which was once his favorite resort. Since then it had participated in the terrible transformation already wrought in the valley by the railroad. A deep cutting through one of the grassy hills had been made for the line that now crossed the lower arc of the amphitheatre.

His conjecture was justified on entering it by the appearance of a shadowy horseman in full career round the circle, and he had no difficulty in recognizing Pereo. As there was no other exit than the one by which he came, the other being inaccessible by reason of the railroad track, he calmly watched him twice make the circuit of the arena, ready to ride towards him when he showed symptoms of slackening his speed.

Suddenly he became aware of some strange exercise on the part of the mysterious rider; and, as he swept by on the nearer side of the circle, he saw that he was throwing a lasso! A horrible thought that he was witnessing an insane rehearsal of the murder of his father flashed across his mind.

A far-off whistle from the distant woods recalled him to his calmer senses at the same moment that it seemed also to check the evolutions of the furious rider. Guest felt confident that the wretched man could not escape him now. It was the approaching train, whose appearance would undoubtedly frighten Pereo toward the entrance of the little valley guarded by him. The hill-side was already alive with the clattering echoes of the oncoming monster, when, to his horror, he saw the madman advancing rapidly towards the cutting. He put spurs to his horse, and started in pursuit; but the train was already emerging from the narrow passage, followed by the furious rider, who had wheeled abreast of the engine, and was, for a moment or two, madly keeping up with it. Guest shouted to him, but his voice was lost in the roar of the rushing caravan.

Something seemed to fly from Pereo's hand. The next moment the train had passed; rider and horse, crushed and battered out of all life, were rolling in the ditch, while the murderer's empty saddle dangled at the end of a lasso, caught on the smoke-stack of one of the murdered man's avenging improvements!

*****

The marriage of Maruja and the son of the late Dr. West was received in the valley of San Antonio as one of the most admirably conceived and skillfully matured plans of that lamented genius. There were many who were ready to state that the Doctor had confided it to them years before; and it was generally accepted that the widow Saltonstall had been simply made a trustee for the benefit of the prospective young couple. Only one person perhaps, did not entirely accept these views; it was Mr. James Price—otherwise known as Aladdin. In later years, he is said to have stated authoritatively "that the only combination in business that was uncertain—was man and woman."

ABOUT THE AUTHOR

 **Francis Bret Harte** (August 25, 1836–May 6, 1902) was an American author and poet, best remembered for his accounts of pioneering life in California.

Born in Albany, New York, Harte moved to California in 1853, later working there in a number of capacities, including miner, teacher, messenger, and journalist. He spent part of his life in the northern California coast town now known as Arcata, at the time it was just a mining camp on Humboldt Bay.

His first literary efforts, including poetry and prose, appeared in The Californian, an early literary journal edited by Charles Henry Webb. In 1868 he became editor of The Overland Monthly, another new literary magazine, but this one more in tune with the pioneering spirit of excitement in California. His story, "The Luck of Roaring Camp," appeared in the magazine's second edition, propelling Harte to nationwide fame.

As an established literary figure, he was appointed to the position of United States Consul in the town of Krefeld, Germany in 1878 and Glasgow in 1880. In 1885 he settled in London. During the thirty years he spent in Europe, he never abandoned writing, and maintained a prodigious output of stories that retained the freshness of his earlier work. He died in England in 1902.

Other books by this author

Openings in the Old Trail
Sally Dows and Other Stories
Stories in Light and Shadow
Tales of the Argonauts
Tales of Trail and Town
The Three Partners
Under the Redwoods
By Shore and Sedge
Colonel Starbottle's Client and Other Stories
Clarence
Cressy
Devil's Ford
Frontier Stories
In a Hollow of the Hills
In the Carquinez Woods
Jeff Briggs's Love Story
Snow-Bound at Eagle's
The Argonauts of North Liberty
The Bell-Ringer of Angel's and Other Stories
The Crusade of the Excelsior
The Story of a Mine

Choose from Thousands of 1stWorldLibrary Classics By

A. M. Barnard
Ada Leverson
Adolphus William Ward
Aesop
Agatha Christie
Alexander Aaronsohn
Alexander Kielland
Alexandre Dumas
Alfred Gatty
Alfred Ollivant
Alice Duer Miller
Alice Turner Curtis
Alice Dunbar
Allen Chapman
Alleyne Ireland
Ambrose Bierce
Amelia E. Barr
Amory H. Bradford
Andrew Lang
Andrew McFarland Davis
Andy Adams
Angela Brazil
Anna Alice Chapin
Anna Sewell
Annie Besant
Annie Hamilton Donnell
Annie Payson Call
Annie Roe Carr
Annonaymous
Anton Chekhov
Archibald Lee Fletcher
Arnold Bennett
Arthur C. Benson
Arthur Conan Doyle
Arthur M. Winfield
Arthur Ransome
Arthur Schnitzler
Arthur Train
Atticus
B.H. Baden-Powell
B. M. Bower
B. C. Chatterjee
Baroness Emmuska Orczy
Baroness Orczy
Basil King
Bayard Taylor
Ben Macomber
Bertha Muzzy Bower
Bjornstjerne Bjornson

Booth Tarkington
Boyd Cable
Bram Stoker
C. Collodi
C. E. Orr
C. M. Ingleby
Carolyn Wells
Catherine Parr Traill
Charles A. Eastman
Charles Amory Beach
Charles Dickens
Charles Dudley Warner
Charles Farrar Browne
Charles Ives
Charles Kingsley
Charles Klein
Charles Hanson Towne
Charles Lathrop Pack
Charles Romyn Dake
Charles Whibley
Charles Willing Beale
Charlotte M. Braeme
Charlotte M. Yonge
Charlotte Perkins Stetson
Clair W. Hayes
Clarence Day Jr.
Clarence E. Mulford
Clemence Housman
Confucius
Coningsby Dawson
Cornelis DeWitt Wilcox
Cyril Burleigh
D. H. Lawrence
Daniel Defoe
David Garnett
Dinah Craik
Don Carlos Janes
Donald Keyhoe
Dorothy Kilner
Dougan Clark
Douglas Fairbanks
E. Nesbit
E. P. Roe
E. Phillips Oppenheim
E. S. Brooks
Earl Barnes
Edgar Rice Burroughs
Edith Van Dyne
Edith Wharton

Edward Everett Hale
Edward J. O'Biren
Edward S. Ellis
Edwin L. Arnold
Eleanor Atkins
Eleanor Hallowell Abbott
Eliot Gregory
Elizabeth Gaskell
Elizabeth McCracken
Elizabeth Von Arnim
Ellem Key
Emerson Hough
Emilie F. Carlen
Emily Bronte
Emily Dickinson
Enid Bagnold
Enilor Macartney Lane
Erasmus W. Jones
Ernie Howard Pie
Ethel May Dell
Ethel Turner
Ethel Watts Mumford
Eugene Sue
Eugenie Foa
Eugene Wood
Eustace Hale Ball
Evelyn Everett-green
Everard Cotes
F. H. Cheley
F. J. Cross
F. Marion Crawford
Fannie E. Newberry
Federick Austin Ogg
Ferdinand Ossendowski
Fergus Hume
Florence A. Kilpatrick
Fremont B. Deering
Francis Bacon
Francis Darwin
Frances Hodgson Burnett
Frances Parkinson Keyes
Frank Gee Patchin
Frank Harris
Frank Jewett Mather
Frank L. Packard
Frank V. Webster
Frederic Stewart Isham
Frederick Trevor Hill
Frederick Winslow Taylor

Friedrich Kerst
Friedrich Nietzsche
Fyodor Dostoyevsky
G.A. Henty
G.K. Chesterton
Gabrielle E. Jackson
Garrett P. Serviss
Gaston Leroux
George A. Warren
George Ade
Geroge Bernard Shaw
George Cary Eggleston
George Durston
George Ebers
George Eliot
George Gissing
George MacDonald
George Meredith
George Orwell
George Sylvester Viereck
George Tucker
George W. Cable
George Wharton James
Gertrude Atherton
Gordon Casserly
Grace E. King
Grace Gallatin
Grace Greenwood
Grant Allen
Guillermo A. Sherwell
Gulielma Zollinger
Gustav Flaubert
H. A. Cody
H. B. Irving
H. C. Bailey
H. G. Wells
H. H. Munro
H. Irving Hancock
H. R. Naylor
H. Rider Haggard
H. W. C. Davis
Haldeman Julius
Hall Caine
Hamilton Wright Mabie
Hans Christian Andersen
Harold Avery
Harold McGrath
Harriet Beecher Stowe
Harry Castlemon
Harry Coghill
Harry Houidini

Hayden Carruth
Helent Hunt Jackson
Helen Nicolay
Hendrik Conscience
Hendy David Thoreau
Henri Barbusse
Henrik Ibsen
Henry Adams
Henry Ford
Henry Frost
Henry James
Henry Jones Ford
Henry Seton Merriman
Henry W Longfellow
Herbert A. Giles
Herbert Carter
Herbert N. Casson
Herman Hesse
Hildegard G. Frey
Homer
Honore De Balzac
Horace B. Day
Horace Walpole
Horatio Alger Jr.
Howard Pyle
Howard R. Garis
Hugh Lofting
Hugh Walpole
Humphry Ward
Ian Maclaren
Inez Haynes Gillmore
Irving Bacheller
Isabel Cecilia Williams
Isabel Hornibrook
Israel Abrahams
Ivan Turgenev
J. G.Austin
J. Henri Fabre
J. M. Barrie
J. M. Walsh
J. Macdonald Oxley
J. R. Miller
J. S. Fletcher
J. S. Knowles
J. Storer Clouston
J. W. Duffield
Jack London
Jacob Abbott
James Allen
James Andrews
James Baldwin

James Branch Cabell
James DeMille
James Joyce
James Lane Allen
James Lane Allen
James Oliver Curwood
James Oppenheim
James Otis
James R. Driscoll
Jane Abbott
Jane Austen
Jane L. Stewart
Janet Aldridge
Jens Peter Jacobsen
Jerome K. Jerome
Jessie Graham Flower
John Buchan
John Burroughs
John Cournos
John F. Kennedy
John Gay
John Glasworthy
John Habberton
John Joy Bell
John Kendrick Bangs
John Milton
John Philip Sousa
John Taintor Foote
Jonas Lauritz Idemil Lie
Jonathan Swift
Joseph A. Altsheler
Joseph Carey
Joseph Conrad
Joseph E. Badger Jr
Joseph Hergesheimer
Joseph Jacobs
Jules Vernes
Julian Hawthrone
Julie A Lippmann
Justin Huntly McCarthy
Kakuzo Okakura
Karle Wilson Baker
Kate Chopin
Kenneth Grahame
Kenneth McGaffey
Kate Langley Bosher
Kate Langley Bosher
Katherine Cecil Thurston
Katherine Stokes
L. A. Abbot
L. T. Meade

L. Frank Baum
Latta Griswold
Laura Dent Crane
Laura Lee Hope
Laurence Housman
Lawrence Beasley
Leo Tolstoy
Leonid Andreyev
Lewis Carroll
Lewis Sperry Chafer
Lilian Bell
Lloyd Osbourne
Louis Hughes
Louis Joseph Vance
Louis Tracy
Louisa May Alcott
Lucy Fitch Perkins
Lucy Maud Montgomery
Luther Benson
Lydia Miller Middleton
Lyndon Orr
M. Corvus
M. H. Adams
Margaret E. Sangster
Margret Howth
Margaret Vandercook
Margaret W. Hungerford
Margret Penrose
Maria Edgeworth
Maria Thompson Daviess
Mariano Azuela
Marion Polk Angellotti
Mark Overton
Mark Twain
Mary Austin
Mary Catherine Crowley
Mary Cole
Mary Hastings Bradley
Mary Roberts Rinehart
Mary Rowlandson
M. Wollstonecraft Shelley
Maud Lindsay
Max Beerbohm
Myra Kelly
Nathaniel Hawthrone
Nicolo Machiavelli
O. F. Walton
Oscar Wilde

Owen Johnson
P.G. Wodehouse
Paul and Mabel Thorne
Paul G. Tomlinson
Paul Severing
Percy Brebner
Percy Keese Fitzhugh
Peter B. Kyne
Plato
Quincy Allen
R. Derby Holmes
R. L. Stevenson
R. S. Ball
Rabindranath Tagore
Rahul Alvares
Ralph Bonehill
Ralph Henry Barbour
Ralph Victor
Ralph Waldo Emmerson
Rene Descartes
Ray Cummings
Rex Beach
Rex E. Beach
Richard Harding Davis
Richard Jefferies
Richard Le Gallienne
Robert Barr
Robert Frost
Robert Gordon Anderson
Robert L. Drake
Robert Lansing
Robert Lynd
Robert Michael Ballantyne
Robert W. Chambers
Rosa Nouchette Carey
Rudyard Kipling
Saint Augustine
Samuel B. Allison
Samuel Hopkins Adams
Sarah Bernhardt
Sarah C. Hallowell
Selma Lagerlof
Sherwood Anderson
Sigmund Freud
Standish O'Grady
Stanley Weyman
Stella Benson
Stella M. Francis

Stephen Crane
Stewart Edward White
Stijn Streuvels
Swami Abhedananda
Swami Parmananda
T. S. Ackland
T. S. Arthur
The Princess Der Ling
Thomas A. Janvier
Thomas A Kempis
Thomas Anderton
Thomas Bailey Aldrich
Thomas Bulfinch
Thomas De Quincey
Thomas Dixon
Thomas H. Huxley
Thomas Hardy
Thomas More
Thornton W. Burgess
U. S. Grant
Upton Sinclair
Valentine Williams
Various Authors
Vaughan Kester
Victor Appleton
Victor G. Durham
Victoria Cross
Virginia Woolf
Wadsworth Camp
Walter Camp
Walter Scott
Washington Irving
Wilbur Lawton
Wilkie Collins
Willa Cather
Willard F. Baker
William Dean Howells
William le Queux
W. Makepeace Thackeray
William W. Walter
William Shakespeare
Winston Churchill
Yei Theodora Ozaki
Yogi Ramacharaka
Young E. Allison
Zane Grey